Baustein **Soziales**

Caring
for people

Isobel Williams

Baustein Soziales wurde geplant und entwickelt von Cornelsen Berufliche Bildung, Berlin.

Verfasserin:	Isobel Williams, Berlin
Berater:	Philipp Fehrenbach, Leinfelden-Echterdingen
Projektleitung:	Jim Austin
Verlagsredaktion:	Laura Spratling
Redaktionelle Mitarbeit:	Oliver Busch (Wörterverzeichnisse)
Bildredaktion:	Gertha Maly
Layout und technische Umsetzung:	Petra Eberhard Grafik Design, Berlin
Umschlaggestaltung:	Ellen Meister
Illustrationen:	Oxford Designers & Illustrators
Umschlagfoto:	Gettyimages RF, Hans Neleman

Erhältlich sind auch:

Audio-CD	ISBN 978-3-06-024154-5
Handreichungen für den Unterricht	ISBN 978-3-06-024147-7

www.cornelsen.de

Die Webseiten Dritter, deren Internetadressen in diesem Lehrwerk angegeben sind, wurden vor Drucklegung sorgfältig geprüft. Der Verlag übernimmt keine Gewähr für die Aktualität und den Inhalt dieser Seiten oder solcher, die mit ihnen verlinkt sind.

1. Auflage, 4. Druck 2020

Alle Drucke dieser Auflage sind inhaltlich unverändert und können im Unterricht nebeneinander verwendet werden.

© 2009 Cornelsen Verlag, Berlin
© 2020 Cornelsen Verlag GmbH, Berlin

Das Werk und seine Teile sind urheberrechtlich geschützt.
Jede Nutzung in anderen als den gesetzlich zugelassenen Fällen bedarf
der vorherigen schriftlichen Einwilligung des Verlages.
Hinweis zu §§ 60 a, 60 b UrhG: Weder das Werk noch seine Teile dürfen
ohne eine solche Einwilligung an Schulen oder in Unterrichts- und Lehrmedien
(§ 60 b Abs. 3 UrhG) vervielfältigt, insbesondere kopiert oder eingescannt, verbreitet
oder in ein Netzwerk eingestellt oder sonst öffentlich zugänglich gemacht oder
wiedergegeben werden.
Dies gilt auch für Intranets von Schulen.

Druck: Athesiadruck GmbH

ISBN 978-3-06-024146-0

PEFC zertifiziert
Dieses Produkt stammt aus nachhaltig bewirtschafteten Wäldern und kontrollierten Quellen.

www.pefc.de

PEFC/18-31-166

Vorwort

Der neuentwickelte **Baustein Soziales – Caring for People** ergänzt die Lehrwerke **Keep Going** und **Work with English**, kann aber auch zu jedem Werk, das zur Mittleren Reife hinführt, eingesetzt werden.

Baustein Soziales umfasst zehn voneinander unabhängige Units. Die Auswahl der aktuellen Themen und Texte berücksichtigt die Bedeutung für die zukünftige Arbeitswelt der Schüler/innen. Besonderer Wert wird auf motivierende Lese- und Hörtexte gelegt, bei denen lebendige Praxisnähe im Mittelpunkt steht. Vielseitige schriftliche und mündliche Übungen sowie anregende Hörverstehensaufgaben erlauben einen abwechslungsreichen Unterricht. Projekte, Recherchen, Präsentationen und Rollenspiele tragen zu einem handlungsorientierten Unterricht bei und motivieren zu selbstgesteuertem Lernen.

Die Vermittlung des Wortschatzes für Pflegeberufe sowie die Wiederholung ausgewählter Grundstrukturen der Grammatik haben das Ziel, dass die Schüler/innen sich in der Fremdsprache nicht nur äußern, sondern ihr Fachgebiet auch auf Englisch durchdenken können.

Die erste Unit bietet einen Einstieg zur Erschließung der Thematik in der Fremdsprache. Die Schüler/innen äußern sich dazu, warum sie einen Pflegeberuf ergreifen wollen, und wie sie sich ihre Tätigkeit nach Abschluss der Ausbildung vorstellen. Im gegenseitigen Austausch auf Englisch lernen die Schüler einander auch näher kennen und finden zu einer Klassengemeinschaft.

Die nachfolgenden Units setzen verschiedene Schwerpunkte bei einzelnen Pflegeberufen und enthalten gleichzeitig genügend Anregungen für alle beteiligten Schüler/innen. Jede Unit kann eigenständig genutzt werden und besteht aus

1. einer *Warm-up*-Seite, die in das Thema und den Wortschatz einführt;
2. drei kurzen Lesetexten (z.T. auch auf der Audio-CD) mit abwechslungsreichen Übungen auf je einer Doppelseite, die schriftliche und mündliche Fähigkeiten fördern;
3. einer Hörverständnisaufgabe;
4. mindestens einem Grammatikthema, das sich eng an den Text anlehnt;
5. Anregungen zu Recherchen und Präsentationen;
6. Partnerarbeit, Gruppenarbeit und Aktivitäten für die gesamte Klasse;
7. Fotos oder Cartoons für die schriftliche Erörterung.

Im Anhang befinden sich vollständige Wörterverzeichnisse, *Irregular verbs* und *Useful phrases*.

Zu **Baustein Soziales** sind Handreichungen zum Unterricht erschienen. Sie enthalten nicht nur die Lösungen zu den Übungen und die Transkription der Hörtexte, sondern auch Hintergrundinformationen, Vorschläge für die Unterrichtsgestaltung, zusätzliche Projektvorschläge, Kopiervorlagen und Links zu nützlichen Websites.

Autorin und Redaktion wünschen Schüler/innen und Lehrer/innen viel Erfolg bei der Arbeit mit **Baustein Soziales**.

Table of Contents

Unit	Title	Texts	Grammar	Page
1	Who cares?	• Who goes to Edre? • Are you happy at work? • A friendly greeting and a smile please!	*wh*-questions *yes/no* questions	5
2	The family	• What is a family? • Teenage troubles • The costs of divorce	the simple present the present progressive	13
3	Is anybody listening?	• Children in danger • ChildLine • Violence in the home	the simple past the present perfect	21
4	Mental health and substance abuse	• Mental health – the facts and figures • I'm going to stay clean this time • Sobriety High	future forms	29
5	Childcare for nursery and school-age children	• Our nursery has no walls • Introducing three pre-schools • Our Club	relative clauses	37
6	Pre-school fun	• An action game • Preparing a talk about a placement • A special time at a British nursery	modal verbs	45
7	Special needs	• Does she take sugar? • Living with disabilities • A smart home	much, many, a lot, (a) little, (a) few; some/any	53
8	Food and health	• FAQs about the eat well plate • Eating disorders • I'm sorry, I can't eat that	adjectives adverbs	61
9	I need some advice	• Where does all the money go? • Help! • Safety in the home	reported speech	69
10	Caring for the environment	• Think global, act local • A good, green beginning • Shopping with care	conditionals 1 and 2	77

Appendix

Results for p27 questionnaire	85	Geographical words	123
Unit word list	86	Irregular verbs	124
Alphabetical word list	104	Money quiz	125
Basic word list	118	Useful phrases	126–127

Unit 1   Who cares?

WARM-UP

1 Match the jobs (A–F) with the photos (1–6).

A care assistant for the elderly
B health care assistant
C homemaker
D counsellor
E nursery nurse
F youth worker

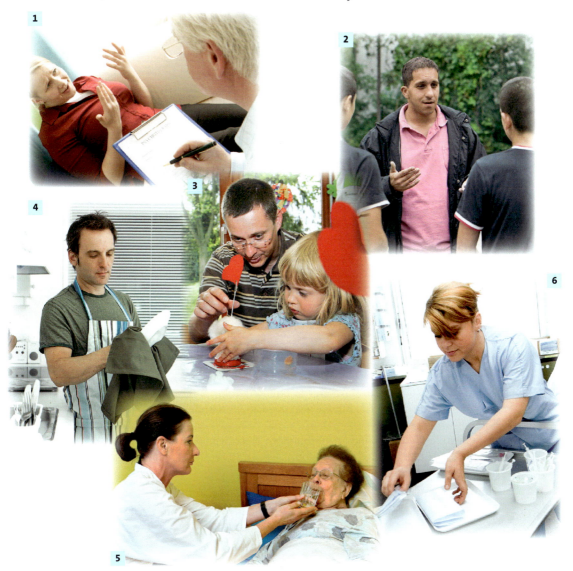

2 List some jobs on the board in which people do things for others. Say what the people do. Leave the list on the board. You will need it for a later exercise.

EXAMPLE   A nursery nurse looks after children.

TEXT 1   Who goes to Edre?

It is the end of the 21st century and NASA has found a new planet. It is called Edre. Edre isn't too far from Earth. There are plants, good air and clean water. Scientists believe that humans and animals can live there.

Earth is overcrowded, and world leaders and politicians want to set up a new world on Edre. They have invited some experts to talk about how to do it. The question at the moment is: "Which skills do people need to set up a new world?"

The politicians and the experts interview people from different professions.
"Why should we send you to Edre?" they ask the farmer.
"I produce food and I know how to look after animals," he says.
"What can you offer?" they ask the nurse.
"I know how to care for people when they are ill," she replies.
A teacher says: "I can educate the children."
"When will these children be born?" asks one of the experts. "Only adults are going on the first ship to Edre. We won't need a teacher for a few years."
A journalist, a factory manager, a social worker and a policeman all give reasons why they should go to Edre.

"How can we decide who should go?" one of the politicians asks. "Everyone who was here gave us good reasons why they should be one of the first people to live on Edre."
"Yes, they did," says one of the experts, "but something is missing from this list. All of these people are specialists but we also need an all-rounder – someone with a lot of different skills."
"Where are we going to find an all-rounder?" the others ask.
Suddenly, one of the experts shouts out: "I've got it! We all know people who are a mixture of teacher, nurse, social worker, ..."

1   Are these statements on the text correct? Correct any wrong statements.

1   The planet Edre is similar to our earth.
2   Everyone is going to leave Earth and move to the new planet.
3   They know exactly who is going to Edre.
4   Only adults will live there at the beginning.
5   None of the people at the interview have the right skills for Edre.
6   The world leaders and experts would like to find a person who can do a number of different jobs.

2 **PAIR WORK** Discuss these questions together and make notes.

A Which skills might the specialists mentioned in line 26 talk about?
B Who is the 'all-rounder' the expert is talking about in line 31?

3 **GROUP WORK** Using the list on the board from the warm-up and the notes you made for exercise 2, choose seven people to go to planet Edre. Report back to the class and give reasons for your choice.

> I don't agree. A/An ... does a more important job.
> Why? Because ...
> A/An ... is really necessary because ...
> That sounds like a good idea.
> I think we have to send a/an ...

4 Complete the questions on the text using question words.

EXAMPLE ... is the name of the new planet?
It's called Edre.
What is the name of the new planet?

1 ... does the story take place? – At the end of the 21st century.
2 ... is Edre? – Not too far from Earth.
3 ... do we need to set up a new world? – Because Earth is overcrowded.
4 ... is having a meeting about Edre? – World leaders and experts.
5 ... are the world leaders and experts going to choose who goes to Edre? – They will interview people.
6 ... is missing from the list of people? – An all-rounder.
7 ... skills does an all-rounder have? – He/She has lots of different skills.

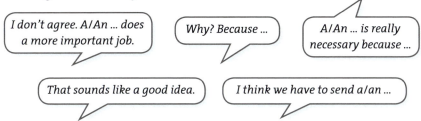

Do you remember?
Question words
- *Who* goes to Edre?
- *Which* skills do people need to set up a new world?
- *Why* should we send you to Edre?
- *What* can you offer?
- *When* will these children be born?
- *How* can we decide who should go?
- *Where* are we going to find an all-rounder?

5 Find words in the text with a similar meaning to the words in brackets. Use them to complete the sentences.

1 (people)   Soon there might be too many ... on Earth.
2 (members of parliament)   Some ... are not very good at their job.
3 (people with special knowledge)   These ... can give advice about things.
4 (jobs that need special training)   They have chosen to work in the caring ...
5 (teach)   People who work in schools help to ... children.
6 (someone with many skills and abilities)   He can do all kinds of things. He's a real ...

Unit 1

TEXT 2 — Are you happy at your work?

caring webzine — your job

Your Job continues this week with people who work as carers. We spoke to Lena, Mark and Eva.

Caring Webzine Why did you choose your job, Lena?
Lena I like helping people when they have problems.
CW Do all of the kids here have problems?
Lena Most of them. It's usually trouble at home or problems at school.
CW What do you enjoy most?
Lena I like doing things outside. In the summer we go in-line skating and swimming and last winter we went ice-skating on the lake. That was fun.

CW How did you get interested in caring, Mark?
Mark When I was 18, I didn't go to the army, I worked in a hospital. I was in the children's ward. I really enjoyed it.
CW So why didn't you become a nurse?
Mark I don't like working at night.
CW What do you like best about your work?
Mark The kids develop so fast and they learn something new every day. I always feel sad when they leave us to go to primary school.
CW Did you have problems finding a position? Is it not a job which is more "usual" for women?
Mark Oh, no. Attitudes to men have changed in caring. There are a lot of single parent families round here – mostly mums looking after their kids alone – and everyone agrees it's good for the kids to have male role models as well as female ones.

CW Why did you decide to work as a carer, Eva?
Eva I like older people. You can learn a lot from the older generation.
CW For example?
Eva They have a lot of experience and they tell me great stories about what they did when they were younger.
CW Are they all physically fit?
Eva No, nobody here is really fit any more. A lot of them have mobility problems and need walking aids or wheelchairs. Some of them are incontinent.
CW Does that get you down sometimes?
Eva No, not really, It's all part of the job so you learn to cope with it.
CW Are you happy at your work?
Eva Oh yes, I really am.

Everyday English
Does that get you down?

to get somebody down
jdn. fertig machen

Don't let it get you down.
lass es nicht zu nah an dich heran

1 **Where do Lena, Mark and Eva work? Choose from the following list.**

> Alcoholics Anonymous • nursery • day centre for the elderly •
> drop-in youth centre • drug addiction advice centre • hospital •
> home for the elderly • primary school • shelter for the homeless

2 **A** **Scan each summary and decide if it is about Lena, Mark or Eva.**

1 This carer gets on well with … …¹. At work, he/she deals with a lot of clients who are not … …². Some of them have … …³ and need help getting around. Some of the clients are …⁴. Dealing with that is not very pleasant but the carer sees it as … … … …⁵.

2 This carer enjoys working with people who have …¹. Some of the clients have …² at home or at school. The carer and the clients …³ being together. They often go …⁴. This carer has a lot of …⁵ at work.

3 This carer once worked in a …¹. At this time, he/she got to know a lot of …². The carer sees that the people he/she looks after …³ very quickly and they …⁴ new things all the time. A lot of the clients are looked after by a … …⁵ at home.

B **Now complete each summary using words from the appropriate text.**

3 **PAIRWORK** Use *do*, *does*, *did* or the correct form of *be* to complete the questions. Take turns to give short answers.

EXAMPLE   … Lena have to deal with a lot of problems yesterday?
Did Lena have to deal with a lot of problems yesterday?
Yes, she did. / No, she didn't.

1   … Lena at work yesterday?
2   … Mark give the children their breakfast every morning?
3   … Eva and the old people at the park yesterday?
4   … Lena and the kids have a lot of fun together every day?
5   … Mark happy at work?
6   … you tired when you get home, Eva?
7   … Lena have a happy childhood?
8   "… I on the late shift next week?" Mark asked his boss. "If so, … it OK with you if I swap with Pat?"

Do you remember?

Questions with **do**
Um Fragen zu bilden, benutzt man *do* oder *does* für Präsens und *did* für Vergangenheit.

Do all of the kids here have problems?
Does that get you down?
Did you have problems finding a position?

Questions with **be**
Am I …?
Are you …?
Is he/she/it …?
Are they …?

Was he/she/it …?
Were you/they …?

4 **GROUP WORK** Choose one of the options below, discuss in a group and make notes. Report to the class.

A   Why did you choose caring? Where would you like to work? Why?
B   What could get you down as a carer? What could help you when you feel low?
C   Mark says: "Attitudes to men have changed in caring" (line 21). Is it true? Which are/were the traditional women's jobs? Which jobs do/did men usually do?

A friendly greeting and a smile please!

How do you feel when you go somewhere for the first time? Even if it's a youth club or a new sports team and you know you're going to have fun, it's still sometimes difficult to go into a new place. It helps if you go with someone who knows the place already.

What about school? Can you remember your first day at primary school? Or, what about the school you're in today? The first day was probably very confusing but how does it feel now? Hopefully after a couple of months you knew exactly how everything worked.

Imagine how it feels to be an old person going into care, a drug addict who hopes to get onto a methadone programme or a homeless person asking for a bed at a shelter for the first time. Imagine how confused and worried they might be.

Whichever branch of caring you go into, it's up to you to welcome the person standing in front of you and get across the message that you're there to help. A friendly greeting is always a good start. And don't forget the smile, please!

1 **PAIR WORK** You are going to hear a carer welcoming a new client.

A Before you listen, decide which of these phrases you might hear.

> Good morning / afternoon / evening. • What's your name? •
> Could I have your other contact details, please? • What's your email address? •
> Can I have your mobile phone number, please? • My name's ... •
> Don't worry. • That's nice. • Lovely.

B Now listen to the conversation. Which of the phrases did you hear?

C Copy the registration form then listen again and complete the contact details.

Name of child	Name of parent	Address
Jane Brown	Fran Brown	...[1] Lily White Road, Ipswich ...[2]
Child's date of birth		
...[3] June 20...		
Telephone number	Mobile phone number	Email address
...[4]	07790 ...[5]	fb.brown@

2 **CLASS WORK** Ask some of your classmates for their contact details and write them down.

3 **PAIR WORK** You are going to do a role play. Do the preparation exercises A and B first.

A Match the verbs (1–5) to these words to produce phrases about activities.

1 do
2 listen to
3 look at
4 play
5 watch

snooker TV darts DVDs
magazines computer games
gymnastics music

Don't forget!
We listen *to* CDs.
We look *at* photos.

B What can you do at a youth club? Write down some ideas.

C You are now ready to do the role play.

Partner A: You work at a youth club in London.
Partner B: You are visiting the youth club for the first time.

Before you start to talk, read what you should say and make notes.
Partner A begins.

Don't forget!
I like to watch DVDs.
I like watching DVDs.
I enjoy playing tennis.

Nach *like* kommt entweder der Infinitiv oder die *-ing*-Form des Verbs.
Nach *enjoy* ist nur die *-ing*-Form des Verbs möglich.

Partner A

Begrüßen Sie Partner B und nennen Sie Ihren Namen. Fragen Sie, ob Partner B das Jugendzentrum zum ersten Mal besucht.

Fragen Sie Partner B, wie er/sie vom Zentrum erfahren hat.

Fragen Sie Partner B nach seinen/ihren Hobbys.

Sagen Sie Partner B, dass es im Zentrum einige Jugendliche gibt, die dieselben Interessen haben. Sagen Sie, dass Sie Partner B mit ihnen bekannt machen werden.

Partner B

Grüßen Sie Partner A und nennen Sie Ihren Namen. Sagen Sie ihm, dass Sie noch nie in einem Londoner Jugendzentrum waren.

Sagen Sie, dass Sie im Internet darauf gestoßen sind.

Sagen Sie Partner A, was Sie gerne machen.

Sagen Sie, dass Sie darüber erfreut sind. Bedanken Sie sich.

4 **PAIR WORK** The headlines below describe some problems in the caring professions. Read them and work with a partner to do the tasks below.

A Einwohner kritisieren Fachkräftemangel in Altenheimen

B Elternkomitee bemängelt fehlende Kinderbetreuung in Unternehmen

C Nicht genug Streetworker für geplantes Jugendzentrum

D Wegen Erzieherstreiks Kitas in 5 Ländern geschlossen

1 Explain what each of the headlines means in English. Do not translate word for word.
2 Say if you think each of them is a real problem in Germany and why/why not.
3 Describe other problems in the caring professions in Germany a) for patients and clients and b) for carers.
4 What could/should be done to attract more people into the caring professions? Think about working conditions, pay, job satisfaction and career opportunities.
5 Why have you decided to work in one of the caring professions? Why do you care? Write a short paragraph in your exercise book. These ideas might help you.

Make a difference   Give children a good start in life   Job security

Use my people skills   Give young people better prospects

Learn about different cultures and backgrounds   Give people dignity in old age

Every day is different

Unit 2 — The family

WARM-UP

1 Make a list of words for people in the family.

mother, father, sister, brother

2 Say who is who in this family tree.

EXAMPLE   Helen is Cahil's mother.

TEXT 1 What is a family?

Sociologists talk about four main types of family:

NUCLEAR FAMILY	EXTENDED FAMILY	SINGLE PARENT FAMILY	PATCHWORK FAMILY
• Parents • Children	• Grandparents • Parents • Children	• One parent • Child or children	• (Step-)parents • (Step-)children

There are two other types of family, the migrant family and the intercultural family. In this article, we look more closely at these family set-ups.

MIGRANT FAMILIES
Migrant families in western Europe can fit into any of the first three categories listed above – nuclear family, extended family or single parent family.

Some migrant families behave in exactly the same way as "native" families in the new country. Other migrant families hold on to traditions, ideas and set-ups which they've brought with them from their home country. Different traditions mean that mothers, fathers, children, grandparents and other family members play different roles in the family.

INTERCULTURAL FAMILIES
Fifty years ago it was unusual for people to marry someone from a different cultural background. Today you see intercultural relationships everywhere. Children in these kinds of families often don't even think about their parents coming from different cultures.

Every kind of family experiences good times and bad times.

1 Some trainees are chatting about the article. Use information from the text to say which types of families they might belong to.

Readers' comments

A VASSO, 16 I don't think we should "type" families. Each family has its own ways of doing things. We are Greek but where the family comes from originally doesn't matter. Whether it's a "native" family or a "migrant" family nobody really knows how a family functions unless they live in that family themselves.

B ANNA, 16 Maybe Vasso's right but I'd like to talk about something else. My dad is always at home when I get in. It's terrible. I never get my own peace and quiet. I'd like to see my mum more often, but she's working, working, working. I get the feeling I don't know her any more.

C KAZ, 18 I know what you mean about not seeing your mum, Anna. My parents are both out at work, so I hardly ever see them. My grandma lives with us. We get on fine, but sometimes I feel that she doesn't really understand my generation.

D LULU, 17 @KAZ and Anna: I live with my dad but he's never around. I'm on my own most nights and I have to get my own meals. You're lucky that you have someone at home.

E SEYRAN, 17 My situation is different. I get on well with my step-mum. I was born in Istanbul: she was born in Berlin. She gets home from work at about the same time as me and we always have a chat. She helps a lot when my dad and I argue. Sometimes I find my dad's ideas too traditional, but with my step-mum's help we always find a compromise.

2 Complete the sentences using the correct word from the box.

brother • divorced • extended • half-sister • patchwork • single parent • half-brother • step-parent • step-sister

1 A … brings up his/her children alone.
2 The daughter of a mum or dad's new partner is your …
3 This family is made up of different generations: … family.
4 Your … is married to your mum or dad but he/she isn't your biological parent.
5 The son of your mum and her new partner is your …
6 Two people who aren't married to each other any more are …
7 The son of your mum and dad is your …
8 When a mum and dad live together with their children from earlier relationships this is called a … family.
9 Your mum and her new husband have a baby girl. She is your … .

3 Make sentences. Remember to put the verb in the right form.

EXAMPLE live / with his dad / usually / Joe
Joe usually lives with his dad.

1 their mum and her new partner / visit / often / Karen and Nicole
2 well with his step-father / Kevin / usually / get on
3 his brother / Ian / sometimes / not speak to
4 Sue / argue / with her half-sister / often
5 never / go on holiday / Tom / with his family
6 I / each family / be different / think / always
7 me what to do / never / tell / my grandmother
8 sometimes / your sister / do you / worry about?

Do you remember?

The simple present

*Sociologists **talk** about four main types of family.*
*Some migrant families **behave** in exactly the same way as "native" families.*
*You **see** intercultural relationships everywhere.*

*Children **don't think** about their parents coming from different cultures.*

Signalwörter:
always · never · often · sometimes · usually

TEXT 2 Teenage troubles

… Sure, my room's untidy but it's my room. I don't want her in here cleaning up. Anyway, she doesn't have any time. She's working evenings this week so I don't see her. Well, except when she comes in here asking about my marks and telling me to do more homework. How can I do homework when she's talking all the time? "Are you getting enough salad? Are you eating fruit?" I hate salad and fruit.
… Yes, I know. She drinks and she smokes, too.
… Oh, yes. She's started smoking again. She always smokes when she's having problems with my dad.
… Right. The phone bill. It's not that much and I don't spend a lot of money on make-up or clothes but she still goes on and on.

… I have to find a different job. I can't do late shifts when I should be at home looking after Leone.
… Yes, I know that it pays well.
… Of course it's hard to make ends meet but Leone's more important than the money.
… Yes, she knows what's happening between me and her dad.
… No, he isn't at home. He's working late again.
… We're seeing the marriage guidance counsellor again tomorrow but it isn't going to work.
… Leone? Oh, the usual things. Her room's a mess. She never helps in the house, even though she knows that I'm tired after work. She never eats a proper meal and I think she's hanging around with a bad crowd at the moment. She isn't doing well at school but she doesn't seem to care. She's either hanging out with friends or talking on the phone.
… Yes, I know they're just behaving like normal teenagers.
… Of course I know that all teenagers go through phases, Mother.

Everyday English

It's hard to make ends meet.

to make ends meet
über die Runden kommen.

1 Use information from the text to answer these questions. The line numbers will help you. Use your own words to give reasons for your answers.

EXAMPLE Will Leone's mum clean Leone's room? (lines 1–3)
No, she won't. Leone doesn't want her mum to help her. Leone's mum is too busy.

1 Is Leone doing well at school? (lines 4–5 +24)
2 Is she looking after her health? (lines 5–6 + 22–23)
3 What does Leone spend her pocket money on? (lines 10–11)
4 Why is Leone's mum thinking about getting a different job? (lines 12–13)
5 Leone's mum talks about problems that aren't linked with Leone's behaviour. Describe these problems. (lines 15–20)
6 Does Leone's mum like Leone's friends? (lines 23–24)
7 Who is Leone's mum talking to? (line 27)

2 Leone often phones her three best friends. Match what they say to Leone's answers in the text to find out who she was talking to in Text 2 above.

🔊 **7** Here are the beginnings of the three telephone conversations on the CD:
1 Paul   What about your room?
2 Marie Is your room still a problem?
3 Lukas It's your room again, right?

Do you remember?

The present progressive

I am
you are
he/she/it is   + -ing Form des Verbs
we are
they are

→ He/She **is working** evenings this week.
  We/You/They **are behaving** like normal teenagers.
  Are you **eating** fruit?

Signalwörter: *at the moment · just · now*

Present progressive mit Bezug auf die Zukunft.

→ We **are seeing** the marriage guidance counsellor tomorrow.
  It is **not going to work**.

---

3 Use the present progressive to ask and answer questions about the pictures.

buy make-up · put on cream · play a computer game · send a text message

 1 Joe
 2 Bob & Pete
 3 Mia
 4 Laura & Kim

4 **PAIR WORK** The verbs in the sentences below are incorrectly formed. Correct them and give reasons for your corrections.

We have to use the simple present for things that happen regularly.

And don't forget the signal words.

1 What's wrong now? Why <u>do</u> you cry?
2 He <u>talks</u> to the social worker at the moment.
3 They <u>get</u> divorced soon.
4 I <u>am visiting</u> my dad every weekend.
5 Teenagers <u>are</u> sometimes <u>being</u> very untidy.

TEXT 3 **The costs of divorce**

Leone's parents are talking to a marriage guidance counsellor. He is explaining some things about divorce and separation. Put the paragraphs in the correct order.

1 "Secondly, don't forget that the parent who looks after the children should get child support. On top of that, if one partner has no income, the partner who has a job often has to support their ex."

2 "Hello, it's good to see you both again. Now, as you know, getting divorced can cost a lot of money. There are emotional costs, too. Everyone involved gets hurt. Let me explain a few things."

3 "Last but not least, one thing which sometimes makes people think twice about splitting up is the children. I'm sure Leone is worried about how things will turn out between the two of you. A lot of children dream about their mum and dad getting back together again. This can make it difficult for the child to develop a good relationship with any new partners that their mum or dad might meet."

4 "As I said, it's not just the money – you have to cope with emotional problems. One of you might feel betrayed or helpless. It's easy to blame the other person for what went wrong. The problem here is that people who are focussing on things that happened in the past don't have much time for the present. Worrying about the past uses up energy, too. You need all your strength to get through this difficult time and get on with the future."

5 "First I'll deal with the financial aspects. Apart from the legal costs of a divorce, the one who moves out will need new accommodation. You usually have to pay a deposit to the landlord. Sometimes an agent wants a fee. Then there are moving expenses and installation costs for telephones, internet, setting up the kitchen, etc. Even small items add up. I'm talking about things like light bulbs and cleaning materials. Some people use up all their savings."

1 Now listen and check.

2 Choose the most appropriate heading for each paragraph. There are two more headings than you need.

- **A** Where does all the money go?
- **B** Providing financial support for single parents and their children
- **C** Taking money from an ex isn't always a good idea
- **D** Bad for the bank balance and painful for everyone involved
- **E** Sometimes it can be a major trauma for the children
- **F** Divorce can be psychologically stressful
- **G** Writing angry letters to an ex can help

3 "Sometimes it can be a major trauma for children." Leone is talking to her friend about the problems in her parents' marriage. Read what Leone says and write a short summary.

> "My parents are arguing a lot at the moment, it's really getting me down. I try to stay out of the way during the arguments. The atmosphere in the house is so bad, whenever I try to talk to my mum or dad they are so irritable. Meal times are the worst – no-one knows what to say.
>
> Sometimes my dad asks me if I know how mum is feeling. I don't like feeling stuck in the middle and I don't know what to say. Whenever I try to give advice to one of them, I feel like I am betraying the other one.
>
> I really hope they find a solution by working with their counsellor, although at the moment I don't feel very optimistic. One minute I'm angry, the next minute I'm crying. At least I have my friends to talk to.
>
> If my parents got divorced, what would I do? Where would I live? No idea. I wish I could help somehow ..."

4 **GROUP WORK** Talk about the questions below.

- **A** Where can a couple who are having marital problems find help in your area?
- **B** What sort of help can they get?
- **C** Describe what a marriage guidance counsellor does. What kind of skills should he/she have?
- **D** If a couple divorce, how can they help their children to deal with the situation?

5 **CLASS WORK** First, talk as a whole class about where we see families on TV. Write some notes on the board.

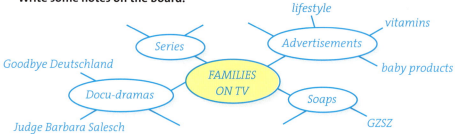

In groups, talk about how TV presents the general "idea" of the family. Are the families on TV realistic, or only stereotypes? Make notes, then tell the class. Here are some ideas to get you started:

> The series Turkish for Beginners plays with stereotypes to show in a funny way how an intercultural patchwork family deals with cultural conflicts.

> Some people feel bad if their family isn't like the "ideal" family in TV adverts.

> In a lot of the Judge docudramas the subject is a conflict within a family. The family members often shout horrible things at each other.

> TV programmes about family life make you think about how your own family works.

Unit 3 Is anybody listening?

WARM-UP

1 Holly is worried. She is thinking about who might help when the baby arrives. Match her thoughts (A–F) to the pictures (1–6). Who might help? How? Who probably won't help much? Why?

A my grandparents
B Mum
C my sisters
D my best friend, Marie
E Dad
F the neighbours

2 Someone is missing from Holly's list. Who is it? Give reasons why Holly might not expect help from this person.

3 This mind-map shows problems which could affect children when they are growing up. Copy it into your exercise book then use the ideas from the questions above and your own ideas to complete it.

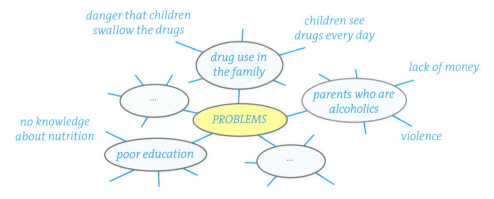

TEXT 1 Helping children in danger

A day in the life of ...

Did you read the paper yesterday? There was a report about a little girl who died because her mum didn't give her any food. A week ago, there were three news items on TV about parents who hurt their children and last month social workers gave evidence in court about a man who had sexually abused his two teenage daughters. We seem to hear about tragedies in families every day. This week, A DAY IN THE LIFE OF ... spoke about family problems with David Webb. David works for Liverpool Council's Children's Services Department. He is a child protection worker.

"Parents are not always loving and caring," David says, "and neglect and child abuse are not new. We hear more today," he goes on, "because neighbours, relatives and friends tell the police and the police inform us about these cases. Some cases make the news headlines but we know that a lot more children suffer than the ones who my colleagues and I meet."

David's team deals with physical abuse, sexual abuse, home alone children and the children of drug addicts and alcoholics. The team works with the whole family if possible, but the child protection workers concentrate on what is good for the child. David sees children of all ages, from babies to teenagers. A lot of the older children have run away from home because of abuse.

"There are a number of reasons for abuse," David tells us. "Poor education, money problems, poor living conditions – it can be these things or a combination of other reasons. Imagine being at home all day with a small child in a tiny flat and no money to go anywhere. Sometimes parents are too young to know how to look after children. A lot of the parents are almost children themselves."

When you read about these cases in the newspapers you see that abuse isn't only a problem among poor families or uneducated people. It can happen in all types of families.

"Every family can be a problem family," David says. "A lot of the time we need to help the parents before we can help their children. Sometimes the parents have problems because nobody looked after them properly when they were children. You can often see a pattern going through the generations. All of the cases I deal with are very, very sad and sometimes the cases are so shocking that I think about giving up the work. But yesterday I sorted out another case and stopped another child's suffering. That's when I know that all the stress is worth it."

Everyday English

home alone child
Schlüsselkind

David's team deals with home alone children. The expression comes from the title of the hit film *Home Alone*, starring the child actor Macaulay Culkin. Although the film was funny and everything was OK in the end, the film made people think about real home alone children and how their situation is not at all funny.

1 **PAIR WORK** Make a list of questions the reporter probably asked David then practise the interview.

What's your job?
Where do you work?

What's your job?

I'm a child protection worker. I work for Liverpool council's Children's Services Department.

2 Match these words from the text (1–6) to the definitions (A–F).

1	hurt	(line 4)	A	not giving enough care or attention to someone
2	protection	(line 11)	B	unbelievably horrible
3	neglect	(line 13)	C	feeling of pain
4	abuse	(line 13)	D	to do something which is painful to another person
5	shocking	(line 40)	E	unfair, cruel or violent treatment
6	suffering	(line 42)	F	looking after someone who is in danger

3 Complete the text using the simple past tense of the verbs in the box.

beat • become • deal with • have • not get • run away • say • send • suffer • tell

David Webb ...¹ us about a case he ...² last month. A boy aged six ...³ from home because his mother ...⁴ him. The mother ...⁵ depressed after she ...⁶ her second child but she ...⁷ any help from her doctor. David ...⁸ the mother to a clinic for treatment. David ...⁹ that the boy and his baby sister both ...¹⁰ from under-nourishment but they are eating good food now and gradually getting better.

Do you remember?

The simple past
Yesterday I sorted out another case.
We spoke to David Webb.

There was a report.
There were three news items on TV.

Did you read the paper yesterday?
Her mum didn't give her any food.

Signal words: *ago · (in the) last week/month/year/century · (a) week/month etc. ago · yesterday*

TEXT 2 — ChildLine

Not every child has loving parents. Have you ever wondered where a lonely, scared child can get help? ChildLine is a 24-hour helpline (0800 1111) for children who are frightened or in danger. It is a voluntary
5 organization which has operated in Britain for over 20 years.

Almost 1,400 volunteers work at ChildLine. The volunteers are all trained counsellors who comfort, advise and protect children and young people who
10 have nobody else to talk to. Every day around 4,500 children call ChildLine. They call about different problems, but the most common ones are abuse (both sexual and physical), bullying, serious family tensions and teenage pregnancy. Some children phone because
15 they are worried about their friends.

Since the mid-1980s, ChildLine has saved children's lives, found safe homes for children in danger on the streets and given hope to thousands of children who haven't known anyone who cared for them. A spokesperson for ChildLine said: "We know that since we opened we have counselled over one million children and young people in Britain."

20 Since 1998, schools and other organizations have worked with ChildLine in their ChildLine in Partnerships programme (CHIPS). Since it started, CHIPS has worked with more than 70,000 children and young people in more than 700 primary and secondary schools in the UK. Because it is so successful, ChildLine has decided to expand the work of CHIPS into other areas. A spokesperson for CHIPS said, "CHIPS has developed
25 resources to help youngsters with special needs, such as deaf children and those with learning difficulties. This year I have visited over 100 special schools and youth groups. Teachers and group leaders have shown a lot of interest."

The CHIPS organizers believe that children and young people should play a part in making changes to improve their own lives. The organization has set up a range of
30 services which help children to help themselves, for example, the opportunity to develop practical I.T. skills through computer courses. It has also helped schools and youth groups with ideas that encourage pupils to support each other.

1 Answer the questions using your own words.

1 Describe ChildLine.
   E.g. *ChildLine is a 24-hour phone service for ...*
2 Why do children use ChildLine? Say what they call about.
3 Who does CHIPS work with?
4 Explain how young people can develop with the help of CHIPS.

2 Complete the sentences with words from the text. The first letter of the word is given.

1 It's a v... group, so a lot of the workers don't get paid.
2 The v... give their time and skills for free.
3 Anne is one of our best c... . She always gives good advice.
4 The place Joey lives in now is very s... . No-one abuses him there.
5 The o... has offices all over the UK.
6 The boy spoke about his problems to a man he called on the h...
7 Daniel has s... n... . He has a learning difficulty.
8 CHIPS provides a lot of different s...

3 Complete the sentences using the present perfect form of one of the verbs in the box.

apply • beat • ~~call~~ • fall • fight • keep • not have • ~~run away~~

EXAMPLE Linda was frightened, but now she is talking to someone on the phone. Linda *has called* the helpline.

1 Julie isn't at school today. Maybe she ... from home again.
2 The child is covered in bruises. His dad ... him.
3 He ... with his brother again. His face is covered in blood.
4 I ... for a job as a counsellor at ChildLine.
5 The baby boy is crying because he is hungry. He ... anything to eat.
6 She ... down the stairs again. She is very drunk.

Do you remember?

The present perfect simple
I have visited over 100 special schools.
CHIPS has developed resources.
People have shown a lot of interest.
Have you ever wondered?
They haven't known anyone who cared for them.

It has operated in Britain for over 20 years.
Since 1998, schools have worked with ChildLine.

Signal words: *already* · *ever* · *for* · *just* · *since* · *yet*

4 PAIR WORK Decide together if the verb in brackets should be in the simple past or the present perfect. Say what helped you decide.

1 Thirty children ... (phone) for help yesterday.
2 He ... (work) as a counsellor for 10 years, before he became a teacher.
3 Mae ... (not sleep) properly since her mum died.
4 The other boys ... (bully) Frank when he was at school.
5 How many clients ... (she / speak to) already?
6 When ... (you join) the organization?
7 Someone ... (steal) a laptop from the club at the weekend.
8 I ... (just finish) writing the report.

TEXT 3 Violence in the home

Sometimes social workers have to deal with adults who are the victims of abuse and violence in their own homes. A son or daughter might hit or shake an elderly parent or a man or woman might attack their partner. Though women sometimes beat up their male partners, police and social workers most often see women whose male partners have beaten them. The American singer-songwriter Suzanne Vega wrote the song *Luka* from the point of view of a victim of domestic violence.

1 Listen and complete the song lyrics with words from the box. You will hear the song twice.

argue • broken • clumsy • crazy • cry • fight • hit • loud • thrown • trouble

2 Choose the correct option, A, B or C, to answer the questions.

1 In the song, who is Luka talking to? A friendly
 A colleague.
 B neighbour.
 C social worker.

2 When do the fights take place? When
 A a lot of people are getting ready for bed.
 B people are relaxing after work.
 C Luka's partner gets back from work.

3 How does Luka try to avoid a fight? By
 A walking around the flat very carefully.
 B going to a neighbour.
 C keeping quiet.

4 When does Luka's partner stop hitting? When Luka
 A gets tired.
 B hits back.
 C starts to cry.

5 How does Luka explain the bruises? Luka says,
 A "I walked into some furniture."
 B "My partner slammed the door in my face."
 C "I wasn't looking where I was going and bumped into the door."

6 What does Luka expect from the person who is listening? That he/she
 A doesn't ask what happened.
 B visits when Luka is alone.
 C tells Luka's partner to get treatment.

My name is Luka
I live on the second floor
I live upstairs from you
Yes I think you've seen me before
If you hear something late at night 5
Some kind of ...^{1}, some kind of ...^{2}

Just don't ask me what it was (x3)

I think it's 'cause I'm ...^{3}
I try not to talk too ...^{4}
Maybe it's because I'm ...^{5} 10
I try not to act too proud
They only ...^{6} until you ...^{7}
And after that you don't ask why

You just don't ...^{8} anymore (x3)

Yes I think I'm okay 15
I walked into the door again
If you ask that's what I'll say
And it's not your business anyway
I guess I'd like to be alone
With nothing ...^{9}, nothing ...^{10} 20

Just don't ask me how I am (x3)

My name is Luka ...

3 GROUP WORK Talk together about Luka. Is Luka a man or a woman? Will he/she ever leave his/her partner? Why/Why not? What might happen if Luka stays?

> What makes someone stay with a partner who beats them?

> Maybe they don't have anywhere else to go.

> There are counsellors who can help.

> Luka will have to go to hospital.

4 Use the text and your dictionaries to complete the word families.

noun	adjective	adverb
	troubled	
clumsiness		
	loud	
		crazily
pride		
		arguably

5 Are you a good listener? A friend is telling you about some serious problems. Read the situations then decide what you would do. Check your results on page 85.

1 Your phone rings while your friend is talking. Do you
   A apologize to your friend and answer the call?
   B answer the phone and tell the caller you'll get back to them later?
   C ignore your phone?

2 Your friend starts to cry and can't talk any more. Do you
   A give your friend a handkerchief and leave the room?
   B describe how you see the problem until your friend has finished crying?
   C tell your friend to take his/her time and sit quietly till he/she is ready to continue?

3 Your friend has stopped talking but you feel you need to know more before you can help. Do you
   A share what you are thinking about the problem?
   B ask your friend if he/she has finished?
   C say: "Tell me more."?

4 Your friend can't find the right words to describe his/her feelings. Do you
   A repeat what your friend has told you in your own words?
   B say: "I know it's difficult for you."?
   C tell your friend how you would feel in the same situation?

5 Your friend often looks at you to see if you understand. Do you
   A keep saying, "I know how you feel."?
   B nod your head and say that you understand at regular intervals?
   C often ask questions and repeat the gist of your friend's ideas?

Unit 3

6 **GROUP WORK** Work in a group of four – A, B, C and D. You are going to take turns to assess each other's listening abilities.

Preparation

PARTNER A	PARTNER B	PARTNERS C and D
Choose one of the situations below and tell the others which situation you have chosen.	Help Partner A brainstorm ideas about what he/she is going to say. Make notes.	Read the situation which Partner A has chosen. Decide together what Partner A might say.

Talking and listening

PARTNER A	PARTNER C	PARTNERS B and D
Talk to Partner C about your problem.	Listen to Partner A and try to help as well as you can.	Listen to the conversation between A and C. Concentrate mainly on how Partner C responds. Make notes.

Feedback

PARTNER A	PARTNER C	PARTNERS B and D
Tell Partner C how you felt during the conversation. How did Partner C help you?	How easy was it for you to respond to Partner A? Try to describe your feelings during the conversation.	Tell Partner C what you think about how he/she responded to Partner A. Explain what Partner C might have done better.

When you have finished, someone else should take on the role of Partner A.

> **SITUATION 1** Your parents don't understand you. Everything you do seems to be wrong. They won't accept your clothes or your friends.

> **SITUATION 2** You don't know where you are going in your life. Everyone you know seems to have their careers planned but you have no idea what you want to do.

> **SITUATION 3** Someone you care about has problems with drugs/alcohol. You want to help him/her but you don't know how.

7 **CLASS WORK** Choose one of the options, A or B. Do your research then report back to the class.

A Find songs which deal with social issues. Bring the song lyrics to your next lesson and talk about them.

> *We found a song by Pink. It's called "Family Portrait." It is about ...*

B Produce a report about face-to-face counselling services in your area. Include the following topics:
- What kind of help is available
- Who runs the service (e.g. church organization, volunteers who have experienced the same problem)

Unit 3

Unit 4 — Mental health and substance abuse

WARM-UP

1 Match the illnesses (1–6) to the descriptions (A–F).

1 AIDS
2 alcoholism
3 depression
4 flu
5 migraine
6 schizophrenia

A People suffering from this illness often feel useless and unhappy. They feel low and don't want to do much. They cry a lot.
B A very bad headache which can also affect a patient's sight. The patient is sometimes sick.
C This is a viral infection. It usually goes away after a week or so. The patient often has a high temperature.
D This is a serious and incurable disease. People get it through contaminated blood, used needles or unprotected sex.
E A very bad mental disorder. Symptoms include hearing voices and seeing things that are not there (hallucinations).
F This addiction affects a person mentally and physically. It also hurts almost everyone who has close contact with him/her.

2 Which of these illnesses do you know about? Why are some of them "worse" than others?

I read that alcohol damages the liver.

My mum gets migraines. She has to go to bed to get better.

There is no cure for AIDS yet.

My uncle had bad depression. He had to stop working for a year.

TEXT 1 — Mental health – the facts and figures

We've all had flu or a bad headache. Everyone has had one of these illnesses so we can all be sympathetic towards other patients who have them. But what about people who are mentally ill? We can't really understand what's going on in another person's mind.

Mental illness can affect anyone at any time of their life. Some patients will recover completely but others won't get well. Some have to take medication to be able to live with their illness.

People with mental health problems sometimes have trouble fitting in to society. They can feel isolated and misunderstood and sometimes won't accept help. Some of these patients will die earlier than they should because they do not receive the necessary medical treatment or social support. Every year, almost 900,000 people around the world commit suicide.

Hundreds of millions of people all over the world have mental illnesses and behavioural problems. Around 154 million people suffer from depression and 25 million people from schizophrenia. The "substance use disorders" are also a worldwide problem: approximately 91 million people worldwide have alcohol problems and there are 15 million drug abusers.

One in four patients who visits a health service in western Europe has at least one mental or behavioural disorder. A doctor at a well-known psychiatric hospital in London commented: "Many patients are embarrassed and won't tell their doctor that they are worried about their mental health. They say that they have flu or migraine – something 'harmless' like that. I think that we miss about 25% of mental health problems. This means that patients will not get the proper treatment. The question is: What will happen to them? The doctor will give them a prescription for their flu or migraine but if their mental health problem is not diagnosed then it can't be treated."

1 Use the information in the text to say whether the following statements are true or false. Correct the false ones.

1. It's easy to understand what other people are thinking.
2. If someone has a mental illness, they have it for life.
3. A mentally-ill patient can often cope if he/she gets the proper help.
4. Some mentally-ill people feel lonely.
5. Mental illness is mainly a European problem.
6. More people suffer from schizophrenia than from depression.
7. Some people are too embarrassed to speak to their doctor about mental health problems.

2 Answer these questions in your own words.

1. Why do some people react differently to people with physical illnesses and people with mental illnesses?
2. Which factors might stop mentally ill people from asking for help?
3. What does the doctor mean when he says that flu or migraine is "harmless"?
4. What do you think health and social workers could do to make it easier for patients to discuss concerns they have about their mental health?

3 Match the facts (1–7) to the figures (A–G).

1 worldwide number of suicides
2 number of people around the world affected by mental, behavioural and substance use disorders
3 estimated number of people suffering from depression
4 number of cases of alcohol abuse
5 number of drug abuse cases
6 percentage of mental health problems which doctors probably don't know about
7 patients in western Europe with at least one mental or behavioural disorder

A	15 million	E	hundreds of millions
B	900,000		
C	91 million	F	25
D	1/4	G	154 million

Talking about numbers!

Cardinal numbers

1	one
2	two
3	three
100	a hundred
110	a hundred and ten
1,000	a thousand
1,000,000 (1m)	a million
1,000,000,000 (1bn)	a billion
1.5	one point five
3.45	three point four five
1:5	one to five
99%	ninety-nine per cent

Ordinal numbers

1st	first
2nd	second
3rd	third
100th	hundredth

4 Match the beginning of the sentences (1–6) with the correct ending (A–F). Then make complete sentences using *will* or *won't*.

1 Take an aspirin and the headache
2 I'm sorry I hurt your feelings. I promise I
3 Don't drink alcohol every day. You
4 Did you really give her money? She
5 Mike's mum is in hospital. He
6 His friend took an overdose of tablets. The doctor said he was very ill. He probably

will/won't

A become dependent.
B spend it on drugs.
C go away.
D probably visit her this afternoon.
E recover.
F say it again.

Do you remember?

The *will* future
Some patients *will recover* completely. Other people *won't get well*. What will happen to them?

Signal words:
tomorrow · next week (month/year) · probably

5 A **PAIR WORK** Talk about what you might do later today or this week. Use *will/won't* and *think*.

EXAMPLE I don't think I'll go to the party this evening.
I think I'll ring Jenny this afternoon to tell her.

B Now tell the class what your partner will or won't do.

EXAMPLE Paul doesn't think he'll go to the party this evening.
He thinks he'll ring Jenny this afternoon to tell her.

TEXT 2   I'm going to stay clean this time

🔴 13   Kirsty Innes works with drug users. One of her clients, Fiona, died last week. Fiona's boyfriend, Mike Doyle, is talking to Kirsty. Read or listen to their conversation and answer the questions on the opposite page.

Kirsty Innes   How do you feel, Mike?
Mike Doyle   I don't know. I'm confused. Fiona wasn't a heavy user, so why …?
KI   Mike, I'm sorry about what happened, but I'm going to have to say it – Fiona was a regular user. I only saw her twice but I know that she did a lot of drugs. The night before she died, she O.D.-ed.
MD   Yeah. OK. She was doing marijuana and other drugs as well. I admit it. She sometimes used downers. She nicked valium from her mum. She needed stuff that was going to make her forget.
KI   What did she want to forget?
MD   Her dad and how he hurt her. She was always saying: "Is he coming back?"
KI   Was it likely?
MD   No. He doesn't know where we live … lived … but Fiona was still scared of him.
KI   She kept in touch with her mum, though.
MD   Yes. She loved her mum, even though her mum let her down. How could Fiona's mum let her husband get away with that …?
KI   The police are going to look into that.
MD   It's a bit late now. Fiona's dead.
KI   I know, but …
MD   We were at the same school. We were great friends. You know how it is – our mates took drugs and we did too. When we left school the gang broke up. Most of them did apprenticeships, but Fiona and I didn't fancy that. We did other things, mainly drugs. Now I feel so guilty, Kirsty.
KI   Now that Fiona's gone … how about …
MD   Yeah. I know what you're going to say. The Methadone programme. I think I'll do that, Kirsty. I don't want to be another statistic. Another dead junkie. I'm going to try again. I'm going to stay clean this time.
KI   The support group's meeting tonight.
MD   Yeah. I know. It starts at 8 o'clock, right?

Everyday English

to let sb down
jdn im Stich lassen

Her mum let her down.
Ihre Mutter hat sie im Stich gelassen.

1 Answer these questions using information from the text.

EXAMPLE   Why is Mike confused? (lines 3–4)
            He didn't think that Fiona would die. He didn't think she took a lot of drugs.

1 Why did Fiona take what Mike calls "downers"?   (lines 14–16)
2 What else might have made Fiona start to take drugs?   (lines 27–28)
3 How was the relationship between Fiona and her mum?   (lines 22–23)
4 What does the title of the text refer to?   (lines 32–34)

2 PAIR WORK Talk about the language in the dialogue.

A There are a lot of informal words and phrases in the text. Make two lists showing who uses which words.

Informal words/phrases	
Kirsty	Mike
did a lot of drugs	a heavy user

B Why does Kirsty use informal words when she is talking to Mike?

C With which of these people would you use formal language? Add more people.

judge • your teacher • police officer • your mum • young client • the parent of a young client

3 Match the informal words and phrases (1–6) to their formal equivalents (A–F).

1 Mike's girlfriend *O.D.-ed*.   A friends
2 She sometimes used *downers*.   B come off drugs
3 She *nicked* valium.   C drug addict
4 Their *mates* also tried drugs.   D tranquilizers
5 Mike doesn't want to be just another   E died from a drug overdose
   dead *junkie*.   F stole
6 He would like to *get* clean.

4 Read these extracts from Kirsty's case notes and then use the words in the box to say what action she took after each meeting.

suggest visiting local doctor (GP) • book place on methadone programme for Mike • find out about mentoring for drug users • recommend moving house and live with new flatmates who don't take drugs

12th April Mike was recently released from prison. He had served his sentence for dealing cannabis and other drugs. His girlfriend has just died from an overdose. Mike is understandably very sad and wants to get clean himself.

4th June Today Mike said he has been completely clean since his girlfriend died. This was confirmed by tests. However, he is suffering from nausea and a skin rash on his legs.

14th May Today Mike said it was difficult to start with, but now he feels completely recovered and will never touch drugs again. He asked me how he can best help other drug users to do the same.

Unit 4

5 Mike and Fiona used to talk about their plans for the future. Complete the dialogue by putting the verbs in brackets into the correct form of the *going-to* future.

Fiona Bell I ...¹ (stop), Mike. I promise. I ...² (speak) to someone at the drugs advice centre tomorrow.
Mike Doyle That's great, Fiona. ...³ (you/ask) about the Methadone programme?
FB Sure. I want to get clean. And then we ...⁴ (have) a great life together. Tell me about it again, Mike. What ...⁵ (we/do)?
MD We ...⁶ (live) in the countryside away from all the pollution and dirt.
FB Somewhere where my dad ...⁷ (not be able to) find us.
MD Don't worry. Nobody ...⁸ (know) where we are.
FB It ...⁹ (be) beautiful.
MD Yes. Everything ...¹⁰ (work out) fine. I promise.

> **Do you remember?**
>
> **The *going-to* future**
> *I'm going to try again.*
> *I know what you are going to say.*
>
> **Present progressive with future meaning**
> *Is he coming back?*
>
> **Simple present with future meaning**
> *It starts at 8 o'clock.*

6 Kirsty tells Harry Jones, the colleague who runs the group meetings, about Mike. Complete the dialogue with the most suitable future form of the verbs in the box. The first two have been done for you. There are two more verbs than you need.

> catch • come • come off • find • finish • have • give • give up • go on • leave • meet • try

Kirsty Innes Hi, Harry. Do you have a minute? It's about Mike Doyle. He *is going to try*¹ the Methadone programme again.
Harry Jones Mike Doyle? He *will give up*² after the first week.
KI I don't agree. He's motivated. His girlfriend O.D.-ed and he's scared. I hope you ...³ him a chance.
HJ OK. If you think so. We ...⁴ a group meeting this evening at 7.30.
KI 7.30? You mean 8.
HJ Not this evening. We ...⁵ at 9.30. I ...⁶ the last train to London. It ...⁷ at 10.30.
KI Right. I ...⁸ Mike and tell him.
HJ Are you sure he ...⁹ to the meeting, Kirsty?
KI I'm sure. He's made up his mind. He ...¹⁰ drugs.

7 **GROUP WORK** Use your own knowledge and information from Text 2 to talk about drug use.

1 Describe why someone might start to use drugs.
2 What makes some people give up drugs?
3 Mike says, "I'm going to stay clean this time." Discuss what a) might make this difficult for him and b) might help him.

TEXT 3 — Sobriety High

Read the text and do the activities on the next page.

How can a student who has come off alcohol and drugs stay clean? One answer is to go to a Sobriety High. Sobriety High recovery schools keep students away from friends who have the same problems. The schools hope that this will help their students stay away from their substances.

One of the first recovery schools was opened in Dakota County, Minneapolis. Jim Czarniecki is the headteacher. "Sending a kid back to school where his or her friends are using drugs is stupid," he says. "Our school helps teenagers stay away from other users. This helps them to stay clean."

One of the teachers explains: "The kids need to learn how to have fun without drugs and alcohol. We have regular lessons like science and languages but students also teach each other how to live without substance abuse." There are about 20 Sobriety High schools in the United States. Recovery results are good and three out of four students complete the programme. Most people who attend a Sobriety High are motivated.

Alicia is one of the students. "If a kid drops out of regular school, he or she might go back later or maybe go on a further education course," she says. "Here, if a kid drops out, maybe he or she'll overdose, maybe even die."

Students attending a Sobriety High have to go to an addiction treatment programme such as Alcoholics Anonymous. The schools do not offer these programmes themselves. "What we provide is a safe environment so that the students have time and energy to work on their rehabilitation," Jim Czarniecki says.

Critics of the schools say that teachers should also be trained substance abuse counsellors. Many parents have said that there should be on-site therapists. But even the people who criticize say that going to a Sobriety High is a better option than sending recovering kids back to regular classes.

Kelly, 16
I had treatment last year then I went back to my old school. But it was just too difficult to say no to my friends. Sobriety High is great. You can have more fun without alcohol.

Gary, 14
My mum and dad are alcoholics and I left home to get away from that. Living on the streets is hard, though, so I started doing drugs. I feel safe at Sobriety High. I'm motivated. I'm going to stay clean and I'm never going back to my home town again.

1 Use the text to answer the questions.

1 Explain the function of a recovery school.
2 Where was one of the first Sobriety High schools opened?
3 The students learn normal school subjects. What else do they have to learn?
4 Describe what might happen to students who leave Sobriety High before the programme is finished.
5 Outline the critics' views on recovery schools.
6 Why are Gary and Kelly at Sobriety High?

2 These people all have something to say about Sobriety High. Who says what?

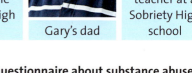

1 Lucy, a new student
2 Megan, a student who has been on the programme for 6 months
3 Patsy Fuller, a critic of the Sobriety High idea
4 Gary's dad
5 Joe Stevens, a teacher at a Sobriety High school

3 CLASS WORK You are going to produce a questionnaire about substance abuse among a specific age group or target group. Do each of the steps below.

A **Brainstorming – whole class.** First, decide on your target group. Then brainstorm the areas you would like to find out about. Here are some ideas you might like to use:
– How people get started on substances.
– What they use.
– Where they use it.

B **Making lists – groups of three.** Brainstorm different substances. Sort them into different categories. Compare your lists with another group and decide if you would like to add anything.

C **Making up questions – groups of three.** Write the questions you would like to ask. Give your questions to another group. Can they think of anything else?

D **Compiling the questionnaire – groups of three.** Write a paragraph stating what the questionnaire is about and saying who it is aimed at. Now write your questions.

E **Evaluating the questionnaires – whole class.** Talk about all the questionnaires. Which are the best/most interesting questions? Put them together to make one "top" questionnaire.

If you decide to distribute the questionnaire, add a note thanking anyone who completes it. State that all completed questionnaires will be treated confidentially. Remember! No-one should be able to find out how people have answered.

Unit 5 — Childcare for nursery and school-age children

WARM-UP

1 Match the German terms for these places of childcare to the English terms and their descriptions (A–F).

1. *Integrationskindergarten*
2. *Kindergarten*
3. *KiTa/Kindertagesstätte*
4. *Krabbelgruppe*
5. *Kinderkrippe*
6. *Zweisprachiger Kindergarten*

A **day nursery / daycare centre:** a place of childcare and education for babies to primary school children

B **kindergarten / pre-school:** a place for three to six year olds to prepare children for school

C **bilingual pre-school:** a special type of pre-school where carers and children use two different languages

D **playgroup:** a group for babies and toddlers to play together a few times a week (often with their parents)

E **mixed/integrated kindergarten:** this care centre is for both able-bodied and disabled children

F **crèche / day nursery:** a place of childcare for very young children (up to three years old)

2 A Which type of pre-school did you go to? What did you like/not like about it?

B What might influence a parent's choice of pre-school care?

Example location
*   opening times*

C These parents (1–4) would like to send their children to special types of pre-school. Read what they are looking for and choose the most appropriate pre-school from the box.

> bilingual pre-school · international school · Montessori nursery · Waldorf school · wood kindergarten

1 *We want our kids to play outside as much as possible.*

2 *I'm from London and my partner's from Berlin. We'd like the children to use English and German at pre-school.*

3 *Children should develop their artistic and creative sides first. Academic achievement can come later.*

4 *We're looking for a place where teachers don't really "teach" but show the children by example and let them follow. Teaching materials should help children learn by finding out things for themselves.*

TEXT 1 — Our nursery has no walls

The nursery in Newtown is for children aged 2 to 5 years. It's called *The Nursery Garden* but it's not a "garden" in the real sense of the word and the children do not have any of the typical "nursery" toys to play with. Instead, they meet in a wood and play with the toys which nature provides – sticks, leaves, mud and rainwater. The children do everything outside. Newtown is one of the coldest places in Britain but the kids who go to *The Nursery Garden* don't mind the weather.

Julie Hall is one of the nursery nurses. "Being outside in all kinds of weather builds up the children's immune systems," she explains. "As long as the children wear warm, waterproof clothes, they don't mind the weather." One of the boys says, "When it gets really cold we play running games. That keeps us warm."

Cold weather is not a problem, but what about the dangers? "The children know which plants are dangerous and that they mustn't touch them," says one of the other nursery nurses. "Children are too protected nowadays," he continues. "Of course, no one wants the kids to get hurt, but they've also got to learn about the natural world around them."

A parent who is a paediatrician says, "Childhood obesity is a big problem today. One of the things which makes children overweight is not getting enough exercise. The children here run about all day. There are no overweight children here."

Some of the children used to go to "normal" nurseries. "There wasn't much outdoor space and the kids were frustrated," says one of the dads. "They came home with a lot of aggression. They are more relaxed now and they also have a lot more confidence. They bring home leaves and flowers and tell me all about the things that they do. It's funny," he says, "it can be raining all day, but when they get home they don't even mention the weather."

1 Complete the sentences about *The Nursery Garden* with the most appropriate ending.

1. The children play
   - A in a garden.
   - B among trees.
   - C in a hall.

2. They play with
   - A the usual kinds of toys.
   - B toys which are specially made for under-fives.
   - C natural things.

3. When the weather is cold, the children
   - A stay at home.
   - B dress properly and do activities which keep them warm.
   - C visit Newtown.

4. The nursery nurses
   - A are confident that the children aren't in danger.
   - B worry that the children might eat something bad and get sick.
   - C know what to do if someone is ill.

5. Overweight children
   - A do special activities.
   - B don't exist.
   - C do exercises.

6. The parents are happy because their children are
   - A losing weight.
   - B developing well.
   - C learning how to make things.

2 Use words from the text to replace the words in *italics*.

1 This is a special type of *kindergarten*.
2 The *things the children play with* don't cost any money.
3 Julie is a *carer who looks after children*.
4 The children very rarely get *injured*.
5 Robin's mum is a *children's doctor*.
6 Children can feel *annoyed* when they can't achieve what they want to do.

3 PAIR WORK Write two sentences about *The Nursery Garden* using the starter phrases below. The first two sentences have been written for you.

1 *The Nursery Garden* is an outdoor nursery. The children play outside all day, even when it is cold and wet.
2 The children play with things …
3 When the weather is bad, the children …
4 They learn about …
5 Because they run about a lot, the children …
6 Some of the children used to get angry but now …

Do you remember?

Relative clauses
*The kids **who** go to **The Nursery Garden** don't mind the weather. (**who** = person)*
*One of things **which** make children overweight is not getting enough exercise. (**which** = thing)*
*They talk about the things **that** they do. (**that** = thing)*

Man kann das Relativpronomen weglassen, wenn im Nebensatz ein neues Subjekt auftaucht.
*They play with the toys (**which**) nature provides.*

4 Write definitions by linking a person or a thing (1–6) to a description (A–F).

A …

1	childminder		A	people watch in the theatre.
2	game	is a person/thing	B	most people love to hear.
3	social worker	who	C	looks after other people's children.
4	dietician	which/that	D	people play.
5	play		E	knows about good nutrition.
6	story		F	helps people with problems.

5 Complete the sentences with relative clauses.

1 They liked the toys. The parents gave them to the nursery.
2 Julie helped the little boy. He was crying.
3 We collected the leaves. The leaves lay under the trees.
4 It's OK to climb trees. The trees have strong branches.
5 He spoke to the assistants. They work at the nursery.
6 Are these plants poisonous? Ask the nursery nurse. She knows about the plants.

TEXT 2 Introducing three pre-schools

Yasmin, Paul and Fiona are pre-school teaching assistants. Read or listen to what they say about their work.

Yasmin

I work at a Montessori school. I know it sounds strange, but Maria Montessori believed that an educator shouldn't teach. She said that children should learn to help themselves. At Montessori schools, the children do things when they're ready. They start to read when they are about four then, later, they do mathematics with blocks and rods. We have a lot of rugs and pillows on the floor where the children sit quietly. They can learn for long periods of time. The children don't get tired because they are learning in a relaxed and happy way.

Paul

We don't push the children at Waldorf schools just because adults think they should achieve certain goals. We believe that education should help a child develop physically, mentally and emotionally when they are ready. Rudolf Steiner developed methods of education which really work. He believed that children should be able to write before they can read and they shouldn't start to read till they're about seven. Pre-school children learn a lot through imitation. They have a great imagination at that age, too. What I like best about this job is helping the kids develop a sense of wonder.

Fiona

This is a small, community-based, non-profit centre. The management committee is made up of staff and parents. The parents don't just "dump" their kids here like they do in a lot of places, they are actually involved in the nursery. It's very important for children to have contact with other age groups so we make sure the babies, toddlers and pre-schoolers all come together at some point during the day. This helps children to develop their communication skills and it teaches them consideration for others. It also allows staff to get to know all the children at the centre and work as a team.

1 These statements are false. Correct them using information from the text.

1. Teachers at Montessori schools do everything for the children.
2. At a Montessori school, the first thing the children learn is how to count.
3. According to Steiner, children should work towards set goals.
4. Nobody encourages children to think creatively at Waldorf schools.
5. The staff at Fiona's nursery don't know the children's parents very well.
6. At Fiona's nursery, the different age groups are always kept apart.

2 **Listen to another carer describing one of the pre-schools mentioned above. Which one is it?**

3 **Describe the photos. Use these phrases to help you get started:**

In photo … we can see … The children are … This shows … I think that …

4 **GROUP WORK** **You are going to do a role play in groups of four.**

Partners A and B work in pre-school education.
Partners X and Y are looking for somewhere to send their child.

Preparation (Partners A and B)
You are both pre-school teaching assistants.
You are having an open day at your school.
Parents are going to ask you questions about the school and your methods.
Decide what kind of pre-school you work in.
Use your own knowledge or information from this unit and make notes.

Here are two examples of things you could say: *We focus on creativity.* *The children have a rest in the afternoon.*

Preparation (Partners X and Y)
You are the parents of a 3-year-old child.
You would like your child to start nursery but you do not know where.
You go to the open day of a school near your home.
Decide what you would like to ask the teaching assistants.

Here are two examples of things you could say: *Our little girl is very shy.* *She likes to paint.*

Unit 5

TEXT 3 — Our Club

Read the flyer then do the activities below.

Our Club offers after-school activities which balance learning and fun.

Our Club offers creative activities like painting, pottery and clay sculpture.

We have different rooms for different activities.
Two teachers are present in each room.

Our Homework Room
This is a very quiet room.
There are three computers and a good selection of reference books.
Our teachers will tell you about the homework your child has done and will let you know if your child should do more work at home.

Our Workshop
Your child can do exciting projects in this well-equipped workshop.
Children can construct models, do physics experiments or make simple pieces of furniture.
Two teachers with specialist knowledge show children how to use tools safely.

Physical Education
It is important that children get enough exercise.
Children do fun sports activities indoors and outdoors.

Weekly Forum
Our Club teaches children to be independent.
We believe that school-age children should be allowed to decide what they want to do at the club.
We encourage children to work toward common goals by choosing weekly classroom activities together.
Your child will learn to be a decision-maker and will learn how to work in a team.

Our Summer Activities
During the long summer break children can take part in our summer activities (e.g. sports day, swimming).

Our Club is open from 8 a.m. till 7.30 p.m. in July and August.

---

1 *Our Club* is a place where children can have fun in the summer and develop important skills at the same time. These 4 main skills are the headings in the table below. Copy and complete the table with activities from the flyer. Add any other skills which you think children could learn at *Our Club*.

Technical skills	Literacy skills	Physical abilities	Life skills (general qualities which will be useful later in life)
– construction of models	– working with reference books	– taking part in summer activities	– decision-making

2 Some parents have questions about *Our Club*. Match the questions (1–8) to sections A–H in the flyer. Then answer the questions in your own words.

1 Can children do homework at *Our Club*?
2 Does *Our Club* encourage children to think for themselves?
3 Is *Our Club* only about having fun?
4 Does *Our Club* have a sporting activities programme?
5 My daughter is interested in making things. What's on offer at *Our Club*?
6 What can the children do in the holidays?
7 Are teachers present in all of the rooms?

3 You are going to set up an after-school club. Do both of the tasks below.

On your own: Copy and complete the following with activities which you think should be offered at your after-school club. Some of the activities can come under two headings.

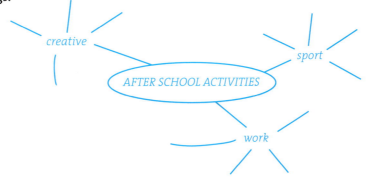

With a partner: Talk about the kind of activities you enjoyed doing after school when you were a child. Add them to the mind-maps you have both produced.

4 Describe the cartoon. What is the artist's message?

5 Mediation

Mediate between a German-speaking visitor to an after-school activities club in London and the club leader.

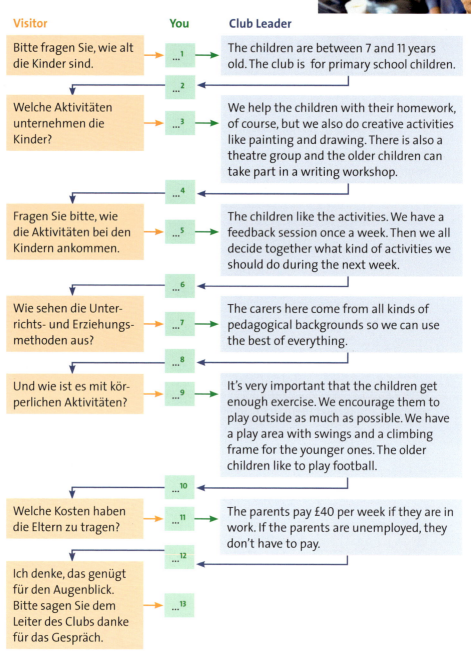

Visitor	You	Club Leader
Bitte fragen Sie, wie alt die Kinder sind.	→…1→	The children are between 7 and 11 years old. The club is for primary school children.
	←…2	
Welche Aktivitäten unternehmen die Kinder?	→…3→	We help the children with their homework, of course, but we also do creative activities like painting and drawing. There is also a theatre group and the older children can take part in a writing workshop.
	←…4	
Fragen Sie bitte, wie die Aktivitäten bei den Kindern ankommen.	→…5→	The children like the activities. We have a feedback session once a week. Then we all decide together what kind of activities we should do during the next week.
	←…6	
Wie sehen die Unterrichts- und Erziehungsmethoden aus?	→…7→	The carers here come from all kinds of pedagogical backgrounds so we can use the best of everything.
	←…8	
Und wie ist es mit körperlichen Aktivitäten?	→…9→	It's very important that the children get enough exercise. We encourage them to play outside as much as possible. We have a play area with swings and a climbing frame for the younger ones. The older children like to play football.
	←…10	
Welche Kosten haben die Eltern zu tragen?	→…11→	The parents pay £40 per week if they are in work. If the parents are unemployed, they don't have to pay.
	←…12	
Ich denke, das genügt für den Augenblick. Bitte sagen Sie dem Leiter des Clubs danke für das Gespräch.	→…13	

6 **CLASS WORK** Find out about pre-schools or after-school clubs in your area. Write a short report about the activities that the children do there.

Unit 6 Pre-school fun

WARM-UP

1 A Scan the texts about child development (A–F) from a magazine for parents. Which of the pre-school children (1–4) do they describe? There are two more texts than you need.

A
At this age a child
- is able to use more than 200 words
- can make lines with a crayon
- might get upset when mother/father goes away
- likes to look in a mirror

B
At this stage in their development, children
- are able to draw a circle
- play well with other children
- can talk clearly

C
Aged ..., the child
- enjoys quiet songs
- can use all five senses: seeing, hearing, smelling, tasting, touching
- cries, coos and grunts
- smiles at a face

D
Now he/she
- can put his/her own clothes on
- might like to hear a fairy story
- may have a sense of responsibility and guilt
- could become competitive

E
This is the age when a child
- might sometimes be angry and violent
- might not share toys
- starts to use short sentences
- can ride a tricycle

F
At the age of ..., a child
- can sit up without help
- makes sounds like a, e, o, d and m
- likes to be cuddled
- enjoys "peek-a-boo" games

1
Don't be upset. He likes you really. Remember, he's only four.

2
It's just her age. She's a terrible two-year-old.

3
He's lovely!

4
She'll be five next week.

B Which two texts do not match any of the pictures?

1 baby – 6 months
2 7 months – 1 year
3 1–2 years
4 2–3 years
5 3–4 years
6 4–5 years

2 **GROUP WORK** Brainstorm a list of things children can usually do before they start school.

EXAMPLE – wash their faces – go to the bathroom alone
– eat without anyone helping them

TEXT 1 An action game

Tim is training to be a nursery nurse. At the moment he's doing a placement at a bilingual nursery. He phones a British friend to ask her advice about something.
Read or listen to their conversation then answer the questions.

Tim Hi, Mary. It's Tim here.
Mary Hi, Tim. Nice to hear from you. How's the placement?
Tim Great. That's why I'm calling. The head of the nursery is going to do my assessment next week and I have to do something in English with the children. I've been thinking about what I could do. When you looked after us, we played games in English. They were great. The problem is that I can't remember any of them! Can you help me?
Mary English games? Oh. I've been out of childcare for years. Let me think ... You'll have to give me a minute ... Oh, I know. What about "Head, shoulders, knees and toes"? Even quite young children are able to sing that.
Tim Hey that's a good idea. We loved that one. "Head, shoulders, knees and toes, knees and toes. Head, shoulders, knees and toes, knees and toes." Erm ... how does it go on?
Mary "Eyes and ears and mouth and nose, ..."
Tim & Mary (together) "Head, shoulders, knees and toes, knees and toes."
Tim Brilliant! Felix and I loved doing all the actions. Fun but simple – that's perfect for this group of children, they are only 3½ years old, so you shouldn't do anything complicated.
Mary Oh yes, it's a fun song. I remember you bending and waving your arms around. That was one of the things I loved about being an au pair. All these games and running about after two pre-schoolers, it kept me fit!
Tim Yes. We had a lot of fun. It got pretty quiet here after you went home.
Mary Well, I had to come back here to finish my training. It was great to do my placement in Germany, though.

1 Correct the wrong information.

1. Tim is employed at a British nursery.
2. He is the head of the nursery.
3. Mary is German.
4. Tim's boss will assess his work next week.
5. Mary works in childcare, too.
6. "Head, shoulders, knees and toes" is a game for older children.
7. It is a quiet game.
8. Tim and his brother liked it when Mary looked after them.
9. Mary was Tim's babysitter.
10. Mary has worked in Germany all her life.

2 A Find the words in the text which match these definitions.

1 Someone who helps to look after children in a childcare centre.
2 The practical part of training.
3 Another word for boss of a nursery.
4 This is the report an employer gives to the school about the trainee.
5 Looking after children.
6 A person who goes to a foreign country to look after children in their own homes.
7 Children who are not yet at primary school.
8 Education for employment.

B Sort the words into two lists under these headings then add more words.

1 people   2 training

3 Choose the correct modal verb to complete the sentences.

1 An au pair *must/can* be fit.
2 Some children *are able to/should* walk when they are one year old.
3 Tim and Felix *could/might* say a lot of English rhymes when they were little.
4 He *may/has to* become a childcare assistant when he leaves school.
5 You *shouldn't/couldn't* leave a young child alone in the house.
6 I *can't/am not allowed to* remember my first au pair's name.
7 Young children *shouldn't/might* understand a lot more than you think.
8 We *might/have to* go out this evening if we can get a babysitter.
9 If he saves enough money, Tim *might/should* go to the UK to visit Mary this summer.
10 Felix *may/should* work hard at school if he wants to become a youth worker.

> **Do you remember?**
>
> **Modal verbs**
>
> **can / be able to**
> - Can you help me?
> - Even quite young children are able to sing that.
>
> **must / have to**
> - I have to do something in English with the kids.
>
> **could/may/might**
> - I've been thinking about what I could do.
>
> **should/shouldn't**
> - You shouldn't do anything too complicated with them.

4 PAIR WORK Talk about things which you should and shouldn't do when you look after babies, toddlers and young children. Here are two ideas to get you started.

You should change a baby when it's wet.
You shouldn't let toddlers run onto the road.

5 Would you like to work abroad like Mary? Why / why not? Write a short paragraph in your exercise book.

If you are interested in working abroad, the European Union offers some exchange programmes for young qualified people. Ask your teacher to help you find out more.

TEXT 2 Preparing a talk about a placement

🔊 20 Tim has to give a short talk about his placement in his English class. He practises his talk on his friend, Hannah.

	Hannah	You wanted to talk about the games you played at your placement.
	Tim	Right. One of the games we played was "Head, shoulders, knees and toes". To begin with, the children have to stand in a circle and then … .
5	*Hannah*	Sorry to interrupt but I think you should say something about the game first. Describe the kind of game it is. Is it a circle game?
	Tim	Well, no, not really. It's more of an action game. The children sing a song and while they are singing, they touch the parts of their body mentioned in the song.
10	*Hannah*	Hang on. Wait a minute. First, they stand in a circle, then they sing a song …
	Tim	Yes, they touch their own head, shoulders, knees etc. at the same time as they come in the song. Listen, are you interested in this or not?
	Hannah	Of course I'm interested. That's why I'm asking questions! Go on.
	Tim	The children sing the song and touch the parts of the body mentioned while they are singing the song.
15	*Hannah*	And what's the name of the song?
	Tim	"Head, shoulders, knees and toes." Didn't I mention that?
	Hannah	Yes.
	Tim	Anyway, the kids liked it a lot. It's a very energetic game so I did it just before they had their afternoon rest so that they would be tired out.
20	*Hannah*	Huh? You did an energetic game just before the children had their rest? And did they settle down OK after singing and flapping their arms about?
	Tim	Erm, well … . Look, can we get on with things?

Everyday English

Hang on.
Wait.
Warte!

1 Do these tasks based on the text.

1 Describe the game. Say what kind of game it is and what the children do.
2 Why did Tim do the game just before the children had their afternoon rest?
3 How does Hannah react to what Tim says?
4 How does Tim react to Hannah's words? Why?

2 Think of activities which you did as a child. Make lists of active and quiet activities.

Active	Quiet
running games	*reading*

3 Tim and Hannah use connectors to link ideas. Scan the text, or listen again. Which of these connectors do they use?

after that … finally … first … now … second … then … to begin with …

4 Put the pictures in the correct order and use the phrases in the box and connectors to talk about a day at the nursery.

listen to a story • play a game • say goodbye and go home • have a rest • have lunch • take off coats and shoes

5 **PAIR WORK** Here is part of a handout which Tim made to go with his talk. The song in texts 1 and 2 helps children to learn the English names for parts of the body. Use the words in the box to label these two drawings.

ankle • cheek • chin • ear • eye • feet • hair • head • hip • knees • lip • mouth • neck • nose • shoulder • teeth • toe • tummy

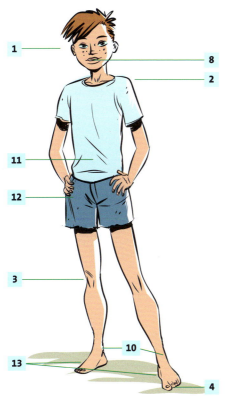

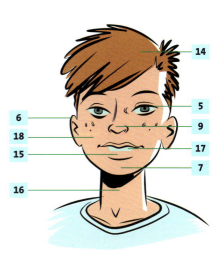

Unit 6

TEXT 3 — **A special time at a British nursery**

Twelve years ago, when Mary went home, she promised Tim's parents that she would keep in touch. Tim's mum has found one of the first letters that Mary wrote.

Dear Marita and Wolfgang

A *Thank you very much for your card and the present you sent for 6th December. I haven't opened the present. I know you sent it for St Nicholas Day, but I'll keep it till 25th for our traditional British Christmas.*

B *We're making decorations and food for our party at the nursery this week. The children love making things. It has to be as simple as possible, of course.*

C *Today we made paper chains. The room is really colourful now. We'll leave the chains up until February. They'll be great for our carnival party. At our nursery we also celebrate festivals from different religions and cultures, like Chinese New Year and Diwali. We make different decorations for those festivals.*

D *Even though it's cold, we go out for a walk every day. We were in the wood today and we collected pine needles and cones for the discovery table. I put some some winter herbs on the table, too. The children smelled the different things and I told them the names. Then the children smelled the things again with their eyes closed and said the names.*

E *Before the afternoon rest, some of the older children sat in the writing corner and wrote letters to Santa. The younger ones painted some of the cones with gold and sparkly paint.*

F *Others were in the cutting and pasting area where they cut out patterns from wrapping paper and sorted them into categories based on size, shape and picture. There were a lot of pictures of Santa and his elves. The children pasted them onto two long strips of paper and we pinned them up on both sides of the nursery corridor.*

G *As you can see, I'm enjoying work. We're having our party next week and I might bake some muffins with the older children for that. I'll put a copy of the recipe in with this letter. What are you doing for Christmas? I really miss you and the boys.*

Lots of love
Mary

1 Choose the most suitable heading (1–7) for each paragraph (A–G).

1 Doing quiet tasks
2 Learning about seasonal plants
3 Baking
4 Making things
5 Decorating the nursery
6 Using scissors and glue
7 Cultural differences

2 Tim would like to bake some muffins using Mary's recipe. Unfortunately, the recipe is torn. Put it back together again.

> **Do you remember?**
> **Linking words**
> First, second, third …
> Then … now … after that …
> afterwards …
> Finally …

Muffins

Ingredients:

250g flour
1 tbs baking powder
50g sugar
2 tbs chopped almonds
some raisins
25g grated coconut

250ml milk
one large egg
2 large bananas (mashed)

A Second, oil 12 muffin tins.

B Then bake for 15 minutes.

C First, pre-heat the oven to 225 centigrade.

D You can now begin to prepare the muffin mixture.

E When they are ready, put the baked muffins onto a rack to cool.

F After that, beat the milk and the egg together, stir in the mashed bananas and pour onto the dry ingredients and mix well.

G Start with the dry ingredients and mix them together.

H Now use a spoon to put the mixture into the muffin tins.

3 Here are some things which Mary and the children did at Easter. Compare them to what they did at Christmas. Use your own words.

EXAMPLE   At Easter, the children went to the zoo and saw chickens hatching.
At Christmas, the children looked at winter plants.

1 Mary and the children hung plastic eggs in the nursery garden.
2 They made a collage showing rabbits and chickens.
3 The children boiled eggs with colours.
4 Mary covered clean feathers, grass and hard-boiled eggs with a cloth. The children felt the different things under the cloth and said what they were.
5 The children made Easter cards.
6 They cut out paper rabbits and coloured them.

4 **CLASS WORK** First, sort the developments described in the WARM-UP on page 45 under these headings. Remember to add the ideas you came up with yourselves.

Child development

Emotional
enjoys quiet songs
often in a "NO! NO!" mood
...

Language skills
cries, coos and grunts
asks a lot of questions
...

Physical
uses all five senses: seeing, hearing, smelling, tasting, touching
can tie own shoelaces
...

Social
smiles at a face
likes other children
...

Now choose <u>one</u> aspect of development and make a table showing the phases a child goes through from birth to age five.

Emotional development

0–6 months	7 months – 1 year	1–2 years	2–3 years	3–4 years	4–5 years
enjoys quiet songs and rocking	likes to be cuddled				

5 Compare and contrast the photos, describing the activities the children are doing.

6 **CLASS WORK** Choose one of the activities (A, B or C) below.

A Brainstorm a list of special days. Choose one and make a list of activities children at a nursery could do.

B English fun and games for pre-school children
Use the internet to find English games which you can use with pre-school children. Collect the material in a class file.

C Decorations for special days
Choose a special day. How could you decorate the nursery? Think of things which the children can make. Describe in simple English how to make the decorations. Keep the descriptions in a file in the classroom. Perhaps you can decorate your classroom for the next special day.

Unit 7 Special needs

WARM-UP

1 Talk about the special needs which these people have.

David Watson
1 cerebral palsy

Emily Mills
2 depression

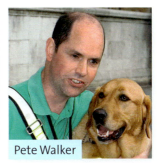
Pete Walker
3 blindness

Cindy Sinclair
4 deafness

Betty Stern
5 Down syndrome

Rose Richards
6 age-related mobility problems

A person in a wheelchair can't go to a lot of places.

The elderly lady can't walk far. Do you think someone helps her with her shopping?

2 Use your dictionary to translate the German words into English.

1 *Beweglichkeit* can be a problem when people get older; they sometimes get very stiff.
2 *Menschen mit körperlicher Behinderung* often use special aids to help them get around.
3 Her *Behindertentransportkraftwagen* runs on diesel.
4 He has broken his leg and has to use *Krücken* for six weeks.
5 She can do her own shopping. She has a *Gehhilfe* with a basket.
6 There's a *Rollstuhlrampe* at the football ground so we can get in to watch the games.

3 Read or listen to the text on the next page. Who says what? Match the speech bubbles A–F to the people in exercise 1 above.

TEXT 1 — Does she take sugar?

A People talk about me as if I'm not there. "Does your mother take sugar in her tea?" I hate that. My mind is working very well, and I can answer for myself – no sugar, thanks – and I can drink the stuff without spilling it all down my front. Perhaps I've become invisible. How many people see the human being behind the walking aid? Not many, I'm afraid.

B I have a few friends and I can cope on a one-to-one basis but if there is a big group, I'm lost. I can't follow the conversation. Eating out can be difficult if there's too much background noise. Every <u>unwanted</u> sound comes through loud and clear on the hearing aid. I don't go out very often. Some of my friends are learning sign language and I really enjoy practising with them!

C My friends say, "Pull yourself together". I know they're trying to help but it doesn't work like that. Everyone gets fed up now and again but this is different. It's a real illness. Not many people understand that.

D A lot of places have ramps or lifts so getting in isn't a problem. The problems start when I'm inside. There's often not enough room for me to wheel around; a few disabled toilets are not fitted out for a person who is alone; if you go to a self-service café, you need someone to help you with the tray. How much can you ask people to do for you? The staff don't always have a lot of time to bring things to the table.

E I earn my own money. I work in a guest house. One week I make beds and do cleaning, the next week I help with breakfasts. Hazel and Tom work at the guesthouse, too. They don't have Down syndrome. We enjoy working together. I like Hazel and Tom a lot.

F Sally is not only my companion and my guide, she also helps me to get in contact with new people. When I play with her in the park, nobody thinks about my disabilty. I'm just another dog owner. I've made friends with some of the dog lovers I meet in the park. When I was ill last year, they took turns to get my shopping for me.

1 Here are six extracts from social workers' case notes. Match them to the people in the text.

1. Proud to be working. Gets on well with able-bodied colleagues.
2. Understands that other people find it difficult to relate to the problem.
3. Has a good social network.
4. Very independent. On top of things mentally but has age-related mobility difficulties.
5. Gets out and about. Accepts that people can't always help.
6. Rarely leaves the house. Aid might need to be adjusted.

Do you remember?

much, many, a lot, a few

There's too much background noise.
Not many people understand that.
A lot of places have lifts.
They don't always have a lot of time.

How many people see the human being behind the walking aid?
How much can you ask people to do for you?

I have a few friends.

2 Here are the answers to some questions. Ask the questions using *How much* or *How many*. Use the *Do you remember?* box on page 54 to help you.

EXAMPLE ... friends? I have a lot of friends.
How many friends do you have?

1 ... trouble? They have a lot of trouble getting about.
2 ... disabled people? Two disabled people work there.
3 ... money? She earns the same as an able-bodied person.
4 ... fun? We have loads of fun at the meetings.
5 ... self-help groups? He goes to two self-help groups.
6 ... therapy sessions? I have three therapy sessions a week.
7 ... time? I need about ten minutes to get dressed.
8 ... disabled parking spaces? There's only one disabled parking space in my street.

3 Use *much, many, (a) lot* or *(a) few* to complete the sentences.

1 How ... hours do you work?
2 He has saved ... of money so he can go on holiday.
3 She has ... of problems but she copes very well.
4 Very ... of us can understand how a mentally ill person feels.
5 I work with ... of different colleagues every day.
6 He doesn't spend ... time with his mother.

4 Mrs Richards (see page 53) is 88. She has been in hospital for the last month. Pam, the patient assessment manager, and Rick, a social worker, are talking about her case.

A Before you listen, make a list of reasons why an elderly person might be in hospital.
B Now listen to Pam and Rick discussing Mrs Richards' case. Why is Mrs Richards in hospital?

5 Choose the most appropriate ending to complete the sentences about Mrs Richards. If necessary you can listen to the CD again.

1 Mrs Richards came in to hospital because she had a
 A broken arm.
 B stroke and a heart attack.
 C fall.

2 She lives
 A with her husband.
 B with her daughter.
 C on her own.

3 She enjoys
 A going out for lunch.
 B being on her own.
 C talking to people.

4 Before she went into hospital, Mrs Richards was
 A having problems with her eyesight.
 B underweight.
 C able to do her own shopping.

5 Mrs Richards suffers from
 A incontinence.
 B dementia.
 C arthritis.

6 The patient assessment manager thinks that Mrs Richards should go
 A home.
 B into residential care.
 C to a nursing home.

TEXT 2 Living with disabilities

1 Before you read, find out some information about the man in the photo.

Definition of *disability* (noun): a physical or mental condition that means you cannot use a part of your body completely or easily, or that you cannot learn easily.

(*Oxford Advanced Learner's Dictionary*)

A Most people with disabilities can and do work, play, learn, and enjoy full, healthy lives. Leading a "normal" life is something which most people with disabilities value. Don't forget: you should talk about "people with disabilities" rather than "disabled people" – the disability does not define the person!

B Some people are born with a disability. Some get sick or have an accident that results in a disability. Some people develop disabilities as they age. Anything can happen and anyone can become disabled. Any of us could have a disability at some point in our lives.

C Doctors say that somebody with a disability has problems doing day-to-day things. Many people with disabilities say that it isn't the disability that makes life difficult – what stops them from doing things is the fact that the world is set up for able-bodied people. For example, wheelchair users can't visit a lot of places because there are steps.

D A lot of countries have laws to make sure everyone is treated in the same way. These laws protect people with disabilities from unfair treatment at school, work, in public places like shops and cinemas and on transport. For example, in Britain, a taxi driver isn't allowed to charge any extra money for taking a guide dog in his/her cab.

E A lot of teenagers with disabilities enjoy going to clubs and discos. If you've never met anyone who has a disability you might be a bit unsure about how to behave. Ask exactly how you can help to make things easier. Before you start doing an activity together, you could ask "Can I do anything for you?" or "Would you like something?" Most important – treat these friends just like any other friends.

2 The first sentence in each paragraph of the text is missing. Decide where these sentences belong. There is one sentence more than you need.

1. As mentioned before, most people with disabilities like to get on with their lives as "normally" as possible.
2. Many people with disabilities don't talk about their problems.
3. Sometimes people and institutions treat people with disabilities unfairly.
4. Disabilities can affect people in different ways and at different times of life.
5. Disability does not mean unable.
6. What causes the problems?

3 **A** Use the text and your dictionaries to complete the word families grid.

noun	adjective	adverb
disability	...	
...	...	physically
...	psychological	...
normality	...	...
...	healthy	...
...	...	with difficulty

B Replace the words in *italics* with words from the grid.

1 The hospital treats people who are suffering from *mental health* problems.
2 She finds it *hard* to talk to other people.
3 The elderly lady is very *fit and well* for her age.
4 It's not a mental problem. It's more of a *bodily* issue.
5 He has a *condition* which makes it impossible for him to work.
6 She gets on with things *the same way as other people*.

4 **A** Complete the sentences with *some* or *any*.

1 Are there ... wheelchair ramps in your school?
2 ... people have disabilities from birth.
3 I've had ... problems with my walking aid.
4 We don't have ... crutches. You'll have to use a stick.
5 Why don't they have ... disabled toilets here?
6 Would you like ... sugar?
7 Do you have ... brothers or sisters who can help?
8 ... friends don't really know what to say to me.

> **Do you remember?**
>
> **some/any**
> Some people are born with a disability.
> Doctors say that somebody with a disability has problems doing day-to-day things.
> Leading a "normal" life is something which most people with disabilities value.
> Would you like something?
>
> Treat them just like any other friends.
> Anybody can become disabled.
> Anything can happen.
> Can I do anything for you?

B Use *anybody, anything, somebody* or *something* to complete these sentences.

1 I'm going shopping this afternoon. Can I get you ... from the supermarket?
2 Is ... listening to me? I have a problem.
3 Mental illness is ... that a lot of people won't talk about.
4 ... laughed at him when he was dancing and now he doesn't want to go to the disco.
5 I can't move my wheelchair. There's ... wrong with the wheels.
6 He's suffering from depression. He can't do ... at the moment.
7 Has ... seen him? He hasn't been to the group meeting for two weeks.
8 I can't find my tablets. Has ... put them in a different place?
9 I don't know ... else who has the same problem.
10 Mental illness is more common than you think. ... can become mentally ill.

TEXT 3

A smart home

A residential care complex in Bristol is using computer-operated technology (so-called "smart technology") to help carers look after their clients in the best possible way.

The residents live in individual flats. The carers look in on the people regularly during the day and answer any calls for assistance. Computers help with the other things that an elderly person might need.

Cindy Green, who is one of the carers, says, "The smart technology does a lot of the things we usually do. For example, it reminds people to take their medication."

Jane Telford's elderly mother agreed to have smart technology installed in her flat. "My mother used to forget to turn off the cooker after she made a meal and I was worried that there would be a fire in the kitchen," Ms Telford explains. "I recorded a message telling Mother to turn off the cooker. When the computer 'senses' that Mother has finished cooking, it then plays the message. I don't worry about her so much now."

Critics of smart homes are concerned about the new technology creating a 'Big Brother' atmosphere in residential care homes. They also point out that technical problems in the computer system could have serious consequences.

People who see the benefits of the system explain how it promotes residents' safety. A spokesperson for the firm which installed the smart technology in the Bristol complex describes the set up like this: "We install sensors which control the water taps in the kitchen and bathroom. Also there are detectors which 'know' where anyone is in the home. These detectors send a message to the computer to switch lights on and off. If the client agrees, the smart technology home can also have a web-cam. Members of the family can then keep an eye on elderly relatives. A basic system costs between £7,000 and £10,000." The spokesperson concludes, "That looks quite expensive but I think it's worth it to know that your mum or dad is safe."

1 Complete these sentences using words and phrases from the box.

1 Smart technology supports …
2 The carers in Bristol make sure that …
3 The smart technology can tell …
4 Now that Ms Telford's mum uses smart technology, Ms Telford feels …
5 People are happy to pay for the system because they want …

> … elderly members of the family to be taken care of.
> … the clients are safe.
> … the carers in their work.
> … the elderly people to take their tablets at the right time.
> … relaxed.

2 Join the beginnings of the sentences (1–5) to the endings (A–E) to describe what smart technology can do.

1 Smart technology
2 Detectors
3 Recorded messages
4 Sensors
5 Web-cams

A start and stop water running.
B can show families that an elderly relative is safe.
C sense where a person is.
D could help people stay independent for longer.
E tell someone to do something.

3 GROUP WORK Would you enjoy living in a house with smart technology? Why/Why not? Talk together and make notes, then tell the class.

4 Replace the words in *italics* with words from the box to produce gender-neutral job titles.

> teacher • officer • person • flight attendant

1 She's a well-respected business*woman*.
2 He was the head*master* at my school.
3 She'd like to work as an *air hostess*.
4 The police*woman* took down the details.

Everyday English

Gender-neutral names for jobs

E.g. A spokesperson for the firm …

Da die meisten englischen Nomen, die einen Beruf beschreiben, keine geschlechtsspezifische Endung aufweisen, war es üblich, einfach *-man* oder *-woman* anzufügen:
spokesman/spokeswoman
chairman/chairwoman

Heute verwenden wir geschlechtsneutrale Wörter:
a spokesperson
the chair(person)

5 Sometimes elderly people need 24-hour care in a residential home. Compare and contrast the residents in these two residential homes for the elderly. The words in the box might help you.

> active • cold • dark • fit • grey • having fun • laughing • lonely • passive • sad • sunny • (un)happy

6 **PAIR WORK** Complete this mind-map showing activities which older people like to do.

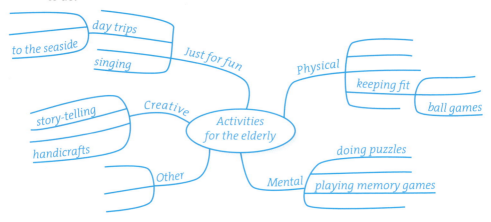

7 **GROUP WORK** You work in a home for the elderly. Plan some activities for the residents. (Remember, some of the residents may not be physically fit; some may suffer from dementia.)

8 **CLASS WORK** Choose option A or B.

A Do a survey of the disabled facilities in a place you visit regularly, e.g. your school or a sports ground. Write a short report and present it to the class.

B Brainstorm problems that people might develop as they get older. Make up a list of questions you could ask an elderly person to assess what help they might need.

Unit 8 Food and health

WARM-UP

1 **A** Copy the headings around the plate into your exercise book. Make lists under these headings using words from the box and other food and drink words you know.

> apples • beans • bread • burgers • carrots • cheese • chicken • eggs • fish • lemonade • nuts • olive oil • pineapple • spaghetti • toffee

B How much of each of the foods should we eat to stay healthy? Match the percentages to the foods on the plate. There are two more percentages than you need.

> 8% • 13% • 15% • 20% • 20% • 32% • 32%

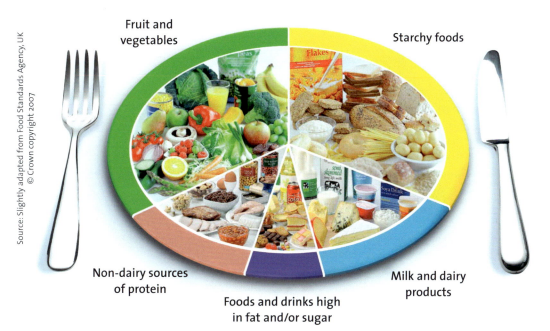

Source: Slightly adapted from Food Standards Agency, UK © Crown copyright 2007

2 **PAIR WORK** Talk about the things you like to eat.

First, on your own, quickly write down a list of the typical things you eat for breakfast, lunch, a snack, etc. If you follow a special type of diet, write that down, too.

Compare your lists with your partner and see where you eat similar/different things.

Depending on the result, either talk together about why you like eating similar things or explain to your partner what is good about the things you eat.

Why do you eat so much fast food?

Why did you decide to be a vegetarian?

TEXT 1 — FAQs about the eat well plate

A poster of the eat well plate will remind you to eat properly. It will help you to eat a balanced diet.

FAQs

- **What is a calorie?**
  We use "calorie" to describe how much energy a food produces when we eat it.
- **How many calories should I eat every day?**
  Here is the recommended daily calorie intake for Europeans. All of these figures are rough because different people need different amounts of calories, depending on their age, levels of activity, etc.

Children aged 2 to 6 years, elderly people: about 1,600 calories	Older children, teenage girls, active women: about 2,000 calories	Teenage boys, active men: about 2,500 calories

- **How much fluid should we drink every day?**
  Try to drink between 1.5 and 2 litres per day. Water, tea and fresh fruit juice are good. Make sure your drinks are sugar free. Things you eat also contain fluids. If you eat a balanced diet, your food will make up about 20% of the liquid you need. A balanced diet means eating the right amount from each of the food groups shown in the plate.
- **Why is everyone talking about "5-a-day"?**
  Cancer and heart disease are two of the biggest killers in the western world. Dieticians say that fruit and vegetables might help to prevent these illnesses. Make sure you eat five portions of fruit and vegetables every day to stay fit and well.
- **Should I completely stop eating foods high in fat and/or sugar, like cake and chocolate?**
  The key is moderation! A healthy diet includes foods from all of the food groups in the plate. If you want to make sure that you are eating healthily, talk to your GP who can give you a health check and recommend the best kind of diet for you. Nutritionists can also advise you.
- **Is alcohol good or bad for us?**
  Some research studies say that a small amount of alcohol (one drink per day) might lower the risk of heart disease. So, should someone start drinking? No. Alcohol is not medicine. It is better to keep healthy by doing sport and eating a balanced diet.
- **What do the initials BMI stand for?**
  Body Mass Index. This is a relationship between weight and height. It is commonly used to measure if somebody has a healthy weight.
  The equation is
  $$BMI = \frac{\text{body weight in kilograms}}{\text{height in metres squared}}$$

  The BMI is a rough measure and does not work for everyone, for example athletes with large muscles or people or are very tall/short.

Average BMI values

	BMI men	BMI women
Underweight	less than 20	less than 19
Normal weight	20–25	19–24
Overweight	26–30	25–30
Obese	31–40	31–40

1 Join the beginnings of the sentences (1–6) to the endings (A–F) to make statements which agree with the text.

1 Our bodies use food
2 Teenagers who live in Europe
3 We should always remember
4 Eating fruit and vegetables
5 Drinking beer and other alcoholic drinks
6 The BMI

A need to eat more than elderly people.
B to drink enough.
C is not a good substitute for a healthy lifestyle.
D to produce energy.
E can help our bodies fight diseases.
F is a rough measure of healthy weight.

2 Combine an adjective and a noun from the box to complete each sentence. The first one has been done for you.

carrots • drink • food • forum • healthy • hot • interesting • junk • meals • mineral • raw • water

1 I love *raw carrots*. I like them better than cooked ones.
2 There's an … … about diets on the internet. I exchange ideas about healthy eating with other people there.
3 Is there any tea? It's freezing outside and I need a … … .
4 You can get recipes for … … if you click on this link.
5 Don't eat too many sweets or too much … … . Those things are bad for your health.
6 Remember to take a bottle of … … with you when you go jogging.

> **Do you remember?**
> **Adjectives**
>
> **active** women
> a **balanced** diet
>
> Is alcohol **good** or **bad** for us?
>
> big, bigger, biggest
> intelligent, more intelligent, most intelligent

3 **PAIR WORK** All of these adjectives are in the text in some form or another. Decide together how to complete the chart.

adjective	comparative	superlative
1 old		
2 active		
3 fit		
4 good		

adjective	comparative	superlative
5 bad		
6 small		
7 healthy		
8 balanced		

4 Complete the gaps using the adverbial form of the underlined adjective.

1 He takes <u>regular</u> exercise and he goes swimming … too.
2 You should be <u>careful</u> about what you eat. Look at the eat well plate …
3 The brothers are very <u>close</u>. They work … together in everything they do.
4 Joe is a <u>good</u> cook. He cooks …
5 He was very <u>hungry</u>. He ate his dinner …
6 The restaurant owner is always <u>calm</u>. She behaved … when the cook walked out.

> **Do you remember?**
> **Adverbs**
> A poster of the eat well plate will remind you to eat **properly**.
> If you want to make sure that you are eating **healthily**, talk to your GP.

Unit 8

TEXT 2 — Eating disorders

Read these newspaper clippings and answer the questions on the opposite page.

1

Pop star Cindy-Lou told a press conference that she had an eating disorder. She spoke about how she used to eat burgers and desserts for breakfast. Sometimes she ate three XXL bars of chocolate in less than 15 minutes and then made herself sick. "The problem started when I got my own show. I couldn't take the pressure and I was using food for comfort," she said. "I would like to tell my fans: Don't become obsessed with your weight. Life is too short to spend it worrying all the time. If food becomes a problem, don't be afraid to get help!"

2

Main conclusions of a recent study into anorexia nervosa in western Europe:
- There are 8 to 13 cases per 100,000 people per year.
- Most anorexics are young, adolescent females.
- Females between 15 and 19 years old make up 40% of all cases.
- About 10% of people with anorexia are male.
- One in ten people diagnosed with anorexia die, half from suicide and half from other complications related to the illness.

3

They can eat up to 10,000 calories in one meal. They are not food addicts, these people are eating as a way to hide from their emotions. They don't want to speak about their problems. They know that their eating habits are abnormal but they don't want to discuss that either. Telling them to go on a diet won't help. The compulsive eater can't go on a diet just like the anorexic can't eat. These people are suffering from complicated mental illnesses and need treatment. Eighty-five percent of compulsive eaters are female.

4

"Orthorexia nervosa" is an eating disorder. The sufferers think too much about eating the right foods. This obsession with healthy food can crowd out other activities and interests. It can also damage relationships.

John, who is orthorexic, says, "I find it difficult to go out and socialize. If I have to go to a restaurant for some reason, I just drink mineral water."

Although orthorexia is an eating disorder like anorexia or bulimia, it appears to affect more men than women. Matt, who has been a vegetarian for 15 years, says, "I'm a healthfood junkie. Five portions of fruit and vegetables a day is fine for other people – I have to eat 10 minimum."

1 **Match the reports (1–4) to these headlines (A–F). There are two more headlines than you need.**

A   Anorexia, bulimia and other eating disorders on the rise
B   Girls are dying to be thin
C   Diet warning for fans
D   Healthy food for fun and fitness
E   Too much of a good thing
F   You can't talk with your mouth full

2 **Say what these numbers from the texts refer to.**

1   3 in 15   (Text 1)   4   1 of 10   (Text 2)   7   5   (Text 4)
2   8–13   (Text 2)   5   10,000   (Text 3)   8   15   (Text 4)
3   40%   (Text 2)   6   85   (Text 3)

3 **Match the cartoons (1–3) to the captions (A–C).**

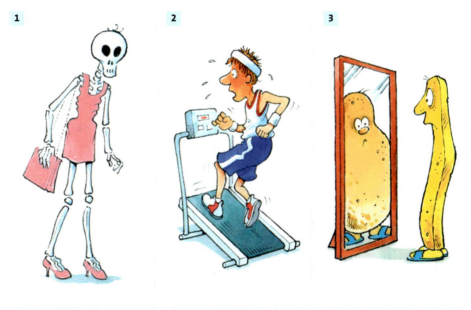

A   I am sooooooooo fat. Where's that diet magazine?
B   At last she has achieved her ideal weight.
C   If you can't change your weight to meet your ideal image, maybe you can change your ideal image to suit your weight. The important thing is to be healthy.

4   **GROUP WORK**   **Talk about these points then share your ideas with the class.**

Which diets do you know?
Where can you get reliable information about healthy eating?
Why do people feel they need to have a "perfect" body?

TEXT 3   I'm sorry, I can't eat that

1 *Some foods can cause us problems. We're not talking about sweets and fats here. We mean the kinds of food which, for some people, can cause allergies. The most common food allergies are to fruit, milk and dairy products (lactose intolerance), nuts and wheat.*

Here, three of your favourite stars talk about their food allergies.

2 *Soap star Melanie Martin has a fruit allergy*
It started in the summer when I was nine. I ate loads of strawberries and I came out in hives – horrible, big, itchy blisters – all over my body. The doctor said that a lot of children suddenly develop an allergy to a certain fruit. Nobody knows why. Anyway, from then on it was no strawberries or other berries for me. But I can eat all other kinds of fruit, so I don't mind too much.

3 *Boxer Tim Hart is lactose intolerant*
I can't digest the sugar (lactose) in milk. When I eat or drink something which contains milk, I get an upset stomach. There are lots of different causes of lactose intolerance – in my case it's a genetic thing. Lots of Chinese people are lactose intolerant. I have to watch my weight because of my profession, so I don't mind not eating dairy products. I make sure I get enough calcium by eating other things.

4 *Rapper Maya is allergic to nuts*
If I go anywhere near nuts I get an asthma attack and I can't breathe. I have to read the labels on everything very carefully. Even that doesn't always help because there could be some hidden nuts or nut oil in a product so I always have my inhaler with me. I get really cool mail from fans who also have asthma. They just get on with it, just like me.

1   **Do these tasks based on the text.**

1   Make a list of foods which the text says might cause allergies.
2   The stars talk about their symptoms. Describe them in your own words.
3   Describe how the stars feel about being allergic. How do they deal with their allergy?

2 The article continues with information boxes about allergies. Match these info boxes (A–D) to parts 1–4 in the text opposite.

A Some people do not have any or enough of the enzyme lactase in their gut and this can lead to an allergic reaction. People from certain backgrounds, for example Chinese, are more affected than others.

B How to cope with food allergies:
- Avoid the foods you know will cause a reaction.
- Always have your anti-allergic medicine ready to hand. Take it immediately if you have an allergic reaction.
- Some people find homeopathic products helpful.
- De-sensitizing might help. Ask your doctor.

C You don't have to starve just because you can't eat one type of food.
- Healthy eating makes you look and feel good.
- Healthy eating can promote healthy skin and hair.
- Always try to have a balanced diet.

D It's quite rare for someone to be allergic to all types. Apples seem to cause most problems, followed by berries and citrus fruits.

3 Complete the text with the words from the box.

No fun food

"Would you like one?" your friend's mum asks as she offers you a homemade muffin with nuts on top. You'd love to eat it, but you ...¹ badly to nuts. Maybe just one little bite? Sorry, no. If you have a food ...², even a very tiny bit of that food can make you ...³. It's better to say no to the muffin and have a nut-free ...⁴ instead. Lots of people have food allergies. They happen when a person's ...⁵ system makes a mistake. Normally, the immune system protects people from germs and ...⁶. It does this by making ...⁷ that help fight bacteria, viruses, and other tiny organisms that can make a person ill. But if someone is ...⁸ to a certain food, their immune system mistakenly treats that food as if it's really ...⁹. The food itself isn't harmful, but the way the ...¹⁰ reacts to it is.

allergic • allergy • antibodies • body • dangerous • diseases • ill • immune • react • snack

Everyday English

watch out!
aufpassen

watch my weight
auf mein Gewicht achten

4 **A** PAIR WORK Before you listen to these people talking about food and health, try to guess which of the things (A–F) they might say.

A "I take vitamin supplements."
B "I make sure we have a balanced diet."
C "I eat a lot of fruit."
D "I have to plan my meals carefully."
E "I try to keep my weight down."
F "I have high blood pressure so I don't use salt."

B Now listen and check. How many did you guess correctly?

C Listen again. Which of these mottos do you hear?

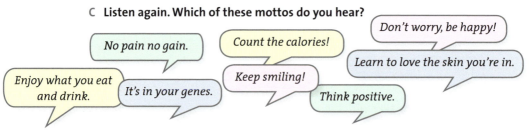

- No pain no gain.
- Count the calories!
- Don't worry, be happy!
- Enjoy what you eat and drink.
- It's in your genes.
- Keep smiling!
- Learn to love the skin you're in.
- Think positive.

D Which of the mottos do you agree with? What is your motto for eating? Tell the class and choose the best three.

5 CLASS WORK You are going to produce two pie charts showing eating preferences of males and females in your class. Do all of the tasks below.

A In groups, brainstorm questions you would like to ask the others about their food likes/dislikes. Include questions about special types of diets. Share your questions on the board and make one questionnaire.

Distribute this questionnaire to other groups in the class. Each person should answer the questions anonymously.

B Evaluate the completed questionnaires and use them to produce two pie charts showing eating preferences for males and females.

C What do the pie charts tell you about eating preferences in your class?

- Here we can see that …
- Whereas females liked to eat more … males preferred …

Unit 9 I need some advice

WARM-UP Make a list of what you spend your money on. If you had to save money, what could you <u>not</u> do without?

TEXT 1 Where does all the money go?

◉ 26 In this week's episode of the popular soap opera *Caring for People* Danny and his mum, Kath, have another argument. What will happen this time? Read or listen to three scenes from the soap to find out.

SCENE 1 In the kitchen
Kath and Danny

Kath (screams) Oh, no! I don't believe it! Danny! Daniel! Come here this instant!
Danny What's up now?
Kath What is this all about?
Danny Where did you get that? Have you been in my room?
Kath I don't go near your room. We've agreed on that. It's up to you if you want to live like a pig. This was in the pocket of the jeans you left lying next to the shower. You know that I always go through the pockets before I put things in the washing machine.
Danny Aw, you're not going to wash my clothes again. You're always saying that my room stinks but that washing powder you use … .
Kath Will you calm down and listen to me, please? What is … .
Danny That washing powder stinks! I'm not a girl, Mum, I … .
Kath I asked you if you would calm down and listen. Why do I always have to ask you over and over again to listen to me? … Thank you. Your jeans are almost walking about on their own so I am going to wash them along with your other filthy clothes. OK? Right. This phone bill was in the pocket of your jeans. Now, I thought we had spoken about this already. You promised me that you would get a pay-as-you-go SIM card. "I'll get a pay-as-you-go SIM card, Mum, honest." These were your very words. But this bill …!

SCENE 2 In Danny's room
Danny and Michelle

Michelle It stinks in here. Can we go down to the kitchen? Your mum said she had bought muffins.
Danny I thought you wanted to only eat healthy stuff at the moment … .
Michelle Well, yes, but … .
Danny I don't think that's a good idea. You'll say I distracted you from eating healthily … .
Michelle No, I won't. Come on. There's something else. What is it?
Danny My mum's really mad at me.
Michelle Did you tell her your credit card was over the limit?
Danny My credit card? She doesn't know about that problem. No way. It's my phone bill.
Michelle Oh, right. Your mum mentioned that you wanted to get a pay-as-you-go SIM card.

Danny That's what I told her. But I like the games I get from the phone network I'm on.
Michelle It's the games that are putting your phone bill up, Dan. They cost a fortune.

SCENE 3 At Ken's Café
Kath and Ken

Ken So how did he explain it?
Kath Well, he said he hadn't had any time to deal with his phone. But, do you know what I think, Ken? I think he can't get out of the contract.
Ken Either that or he doesn't have the money to change to another network.
Kath Oh, no. He's got money. If you ask me, he's got too much money. His dad gave him a credit card for his 18th birthday and he's been buying stuff like mad ever since. I told Martin that giving Danny a credit card wasn't a good idea. I said, "It isn't a good idea to give a kid of his age a credit card, Martin," but he wouldn't listen as usual.
Ken Danny's got a credit card? Uh-oh. Kids and credit cards? Bad idea. They think they've got money, but all they've got is debts.
Kath Do you think Danny's in debt? No, he wouldn't be so stupid.
Ken Well, he's been stupid about his mobile phone. You know, Kath, you can always talk to someone at the Citizen's Advice Bureau. They'd know what to do about the phone bill. It's a huge bill. He might be able to pay it off in instalments.
Kath Yes, you're right. I'll have to do something. Michelle's a good influence on him. I think I'll talk to her about it first. You know, Ken, I said I would kick him out the next time we had any trouble, but I don't want to do that. A mother can't do that to a child. Anyway, he's the only person I've got. I'd be lonely without him in the house.

1 Answer these questions and do these tasks based on the text.

Everyday English
What's up now?
Was ist jetzt los?

1 Which four things do Danny and Kath always fight about?
2 What is the main problem in this episode?
3 Explain why Michelle wants to go to the kitchen. What does Danny say?
4 Explain why Danny doesn't want to go into the kitchen.
5 Comment on the reason why Danny doesn't want to change his phone contract.
6 Describe Kath's feelings about Danny's credit card.
7 Describe Ken's reaction when he hears that Danny has a credit card.
8 What does Ken advise?
9 What does Kath think about Ken's advice?
10 Is Kath going to tell Danny to move out or not? What are her reasons?

2 Match these definitions to words in the text.

1 What you have before you've paid your bills.
2 A huge amount of money.
3 This tells you how much you have to pay for something.
4 The highest amount of money you are allowed to spend.
5 A number of payments made regularly over a period of time.
6 When the money on this runs out, you can't make any more calls.

7   People use this to buy things which they will pay for later.
8   A formal document you sign when you agree to do something.

Do you remember?

Reported speech

In reported speech, the tenses change as follows:

"Michelle **is** a good influence on him." → Kath said that Michelle **was** a good influence on Danny.
"I **bought** muffins this morning." → Kath said she **had bought** muffins.
"We **have spoken** about this before." → Kath said that they **had spoken** about it before.
"**I'll get** a pay-as-you-go SIM card." → You promised that you **would get** a pay-as-you-go SIM card.
"You **can talk** to someone at the Citizen's Advice Bureau." → Ken said that Kath **could talk** to someone at the Citizen's Advice Bureau.

"**Will** you calm down and listen?" → I asked you if you **would** calm down and listen.
"**Do** you **think** that Danny is in debt?" → Kath asked Ken **if/whether** he **thought** Danny was in debt.

3   Change these sentences into direct speech. Don't forget the tense change!

1   Danny told Michelle he would phone her later. Danny said, "I …
2   Ken asked Kath if she would go out with him one evening. Ken said, "Kath …
3   Michelle told her mum that Danny had a problem. Michelle said, "Danny …
4   Kath told Michelle that Ken was a nice person. Kath said, "Ken …
5   Michelle's mum told Michelle that she could easily find another boyfriend. Michelle's mum said, "You …
6   Kath told Michelle that she and Martin had separated when Danny was two. Kath said, "Martin and I …
7   Michelle asked a friend if she thought Danny was nice. Michelle said, " …

4   PAIR WORK   Read the text again and change the dialogues into reported speech. Start the sections like this:

1   Kath was in the kitchen. She shouted to Danny that …
2   Danny and Michelle were in Danny's room. Michelle asked Danny if …
3   Kath was talking to Ken in his café. She told him that …

5   Kath and Danny are talking to Helen Ross at the Citizen's Advice Bureau. Helen helps people sort out their debts. Listen to the CD and answer these questions.

1   How much was Danny's last mobile phone bill?
2   How much is this one?
3   Why is the bill so high?
4   How does Danny explain his behaviour?
5   What does Helen suggest?
6   Does Kath know about Danny's credit card problem?

TEXT 2 — Help!

Youth Café is a website for teenagers. This is part of the forum. Read the threads then do the tasks opposite.

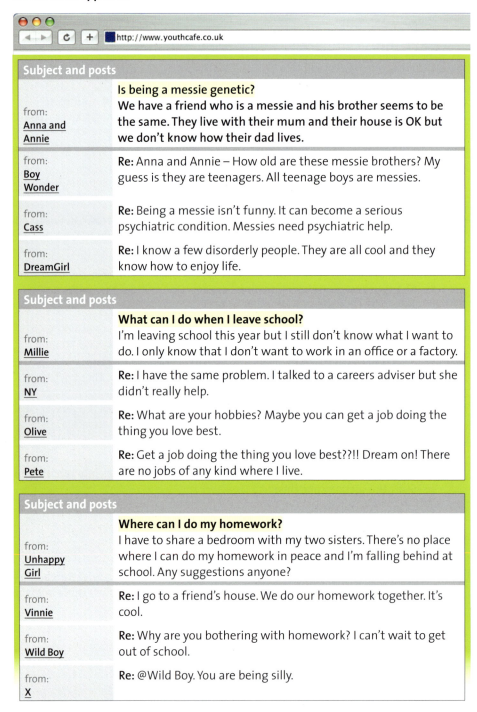

1 The statements below (1–12) have disappeared from the Forum. Match each of them to one of the posts on the forum. The first two have been done for you.

EXAMPLE *1 X, 2 NY*

1 Grow up.
2 I was really disappointed.
3 This is a real disorder. These people aren't lazy, they just can't help it.
4 What are the alternatives?
5 In our town, people leave school and go straight on social security benefits.
6 It's fun working together.
7 Relax. Be happy.
8 I don't have anywhere to sit quietly.
9 I find homework boring.
10 Does it run in families?
11 What do you dream of doing?
12 They'll grow out of it.

2 Change the highlighted questions in the forum into reported speech.

3 Compare and contrast these two photos. What does each of the rooms say about the people who use it?
Use these phrases to help you get started:

In photo A we can see that ... whereas in photo B ....
The main difference between the two photos is ...
One similarity is ...
This suggests that ...
This shows that ...

A

B

TEXT 3 Safety in the home

A

Every day more than 1,500 people aged 60 or over have an accident and need to go to hospital. Burns and falls are the most common accidents and more than half of these accidents happen at home. Here are some tips to help you keep the home of an elderly friend or relative safe. Always make sure that people are happy to accept your help.

B

Did you know that

* 70% of the refrigerators which elderly people use are too warm for safe storage of food?

* 20% of elderly people do not understand why food labels show "use by" and "sell by" dates?

* 80% of the elderly cannot see well enough to read the labels on tins and cartons of food?

This means that some elderly people could be eating unsafe food.

Here are some tips to help the elderly eat safely:

C

Burns and scalds – not only a danger in the kitchen

– Use guards on fires.

– Make sure cookers are switched off immediately after use.

– Check thermostats on hot water tanks.

Burns and scalds are easy to prevent – make sure you do!

D

Slipping and tripping

A lot of people have loose rugs in their homes. Old people can slip on them.
Torn carpets are dangerous in any home. An old person might trip and break their bones.
Old people often don't see small things lying around.
Here's how to improve safety on the floor:

E

Safety first

Many of us think that elderly people are particularly at risk from crime. Even though statistics tell us that this isn't true, elderly people can feel scared. Here are some things you can do which might help an elderly person feel safer:

1 Answer these questions based on the text.

1 The leaflets are aimed at
   A someone who knows elderly people.   B elderly people.
   C carers and the elderly.
2 Explain the sentence: "Always make sure that people are happy to accept your help."
3 Say what these numbers represent and what they mean for old people:
   A 70%   B 20%   C 80%
4 Use information from text C to explain the phrase "not only a danger in the kitchen".
5 When should people change their floor coverings?
6 Who believes that old people are at a greater risk from crime?
   A elderly people   B everyone
   C a lot of people, including the elderly

2 PAIR WORK Choose one of the leaflets and brainstorm ideas to make the homes of elderly people safe. Use the following headings:

Help the elderly eat safely. • More things you can do to prevent burns and scalds. • How to improve safety on the floor. • Things you can do to help an elderly person feel safer.

3 GROUP WORK Look at the drawings and find six things which are dangerous. Use your ideas from exercise 2 to make the home safer.

4 CLASS WORK Choose one of the options, A or B.

A Money management
Do the quiz on page 125 individually.
Now imagine that your monthly income has been cut by half. What would you have to change so that you would not get into debt?
Exchange ideas about how you can make these changes.

B Safety in the home
Assess the home of someone you know well and make a list of things which are unsafe. What should be changed to make the home safer?

5 Do you remember Rose Richards? She had a fall at home. (See Unit 7, page 53) While she was in hospital, Mrs Richards wrote this letter to her daughter. Complete the letter with words from the box. The first one has been done for you.

angry • feels • ~~active~~ • hate • home help • home shopper • hurts • impatient • independent • medication • possible • social workers • stiff • residential home

Dear Louise

Thank you so much for the crossword puzzle book. I like to keep my brain active ¹. I don't feel old in my mind at all but I ...² my old body.

Have young people ever thought how it ...³ to have a body that no longer serves the person it belongs to? A body that ...⁴ all over by the time you go to bed at night? I'm getting some new ...⁵ for my arthritis. It isn't working yet but the doctor says I've to be patient. I've always been ...⁶ . I still want to do the things I always did, but it's no longer ...⁷.

I have to come to terms with this*. I'm in here because I couldn't accept that. I couldn't wait for the ...⁸ to come and replace a broken lightbulb so I stood on a chair and tried to do it myself. My hand was ...⁹ and I couldn't do it and that made me so ...¹⁰ that I fell off the chair. I suppose I was fortunate that I didn't break my neck.

They are talking about putting me into a ... ¹¹ but I don't want to go to a place like that. I want to live in my own home. I know I would be all right. My home help comes twice a week and my ...¹² goes to the supermarket for me every Friday. I would accept meals on wheels. I want to stay ...¹³ for as long as I can.

Will you be coming home for a visit soon? I'd like you to talk to the ...¹⁴ and tell them that I can look after myself very well.

Give my love to Jack and the children.

Love   Mum xx

Everyday English

*to come to terms with sth
sich mit etwas abfinden

6 **GROUP WORK**

A Use Mrs Richards' letter to answer the questions below. Make notes.
How does it feel to be old? What are the general problems that old people face today? Here are some ideas:

People don't grow old, it's bodies that grow old.

It must be very frustrating when you can't do the things you want to do.

She has to come to terms with the fact that she's old.

B Use your notes to write an email from Louise to a friend. Describe how Louise feels about her elderly mother's problems. Say how Mrs Richards' story continues.

Unit 9

Unit 10 Caring for the environment

WARM-UP

1 Describe these cartoons. What is the "message" of each cartoon?

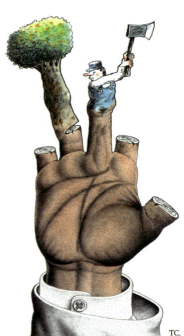

Cartoons used by kind permission of the Ken Sprague International Political Cartoon Competition

2 Match these phrases (1–6) to their definitions (A–F).

1 biodegradable
2 carbon footprint
3 ecological footprint
4 fair trade
5 food miles
6 H$_2$O footprint

A This is a way to make sure that producers receive proper payment for their goods and have a right to decent working conditions.
B People use this expression to talk about the distance the things we eat travel before they get to our tables.
C This is the amount of water used in the production of an object or service.
D We say this when we talk about the total amount of greenhouse gases produced by human activities.
E When we talk about something which has had a permanent and damaging effect on the surrounding environment we can use this expression.
F This word describes a substance or thing which will not damage the environment as it breaks down. Natural bacteria help the process.

TEXT 1 Think global, act local

Saving water

We can all help the environment by making small changes to our home lives. We use 3/4 of our water in the bathroom so let's start by shrinking our H_2O footprint there!

- A four-minute shower uses 60 to 80 litres. If you take shorter showers, you'll save water.
- A typical bath uses about 150 litres of water. If you have a bath, use the water afterwards to water plants or wash your car.
- We use 28% of our water to flush the WC so don't flush when you don't need to.
- When you clean your teeth

SAVING ELECTRICITY

Every year our electricity gets more and more expensive. When you waste electricity you waste money. It's easy to forget the environment. When you plug something into the wall, you don't see or smell any pollution so it seems to be clean enough. But the pollution is there – it's just that it happens somewhere else – at the power plant.

If you follow the tips in this leaflet, you'll save electricity and reduce your carbon footprint. And when you get your next bill, you'll see how much money you can save.

Electricity monitor

1 TVs and DVD players can use up to 90% as much power in standby mode as when they are on. You'll save electricity if you switch off completely. An electricity monitor shows you how much electricity you are using (and what this costs) in real time.

2 If you hang your clothes outside to dry instead of drying them in a tumble drier, you'll save

1 The statements are false. Correct them by using information from the text.

1 People use most of their water in the kitchen.
2 Taking a shower uses more water than taking a bath.
3 The water leaflet suggests that people should stop taking baths.
4 An electricity monitor does not show the price of the electricity you use.
5 It's easy to see how using electricity pollutes the atmosphere.
6 You can save a lot of electricity when you leave equipment on standby.

2 Complete this summary by using words from the text. Gaps 11 and 12 need two words each.

Everyone should think about ways to ...¹ water. Start in the ...². Take shorter ...³ or recycle the water from your ...⁴. You can use it to ...⁵ your garden. Don't ...⁶ the WC more often than necessary.
People often forget about the ...⁷ when they use ...⁸. They think that it's a ...⁹ form of energy and there isn't any ...¹⁰. Remember to ... ...¹¹ equipment when you're not using it. That way you'll reduce your ... ...¹².

3 Make conditional sentences. Add commas where necessary.

EXAMPLES
you use a lot of water / you / get big water bills
If you use a lot of water, you will get big water bills.
The government build more power stations / consumers demand more electricity
The government will build more power stations if consumers demand more electricity.

> **Do you remember?**
> **Conditional 1**
> If you take shorter showers, you'll save quite a lot of water.
> You'll save electricity if you switch off completely.
>
> Verwechseln Sie nicht *if* mit *when*.
> ~~If~~ you get your next bill ...
> When you get your next bill, you'll see how much money you can save.
>
> Remember! *If* und *will* kommen nie im selben Nebensatz vor:
> If you ~~will~~ save water, ...

1 you put cigarette ends into the WC / you / pollute the water
2 you wash your hair too often / it / get dull
3 turn off the tap while you clean your teeth / you want to save water
4 Dave doesn't wash his car / he knows it's going to rain
5 switch off the lights / you are not going back into the room for a while
6 you buy a new refrigerator / it / use less electricity than the old one
7 people consume more electricity / the environment / suffer
8 attach this meter to your equipment / it / show you how much electricity you use

4 Complete these sentences with *if* or *when*.

1 Sarah always takes hours in the bathroom ... she's getting ready for a concert.
2 ... it's hot at the weekend, people will drink more water.
3 He always washes his hair ... he has a bath.
4 ... you leave the lights on day and night, you will have a huge bill.
5 ... you change your contract, you will get cheaper electricity.
6 ... people buy electricity from an environmentally-friendly supplier, they hope to do something positive for the environment.

5 GROUP WORK Do the first part of the task with a partner, then work with another pair.

A With your partner, choose one of the leaflets and add more tips.
B Now talk with a pair who have added tips to the other leaflet. Decide together on the most useful tips for saving water or electricity.

A good, green beginning

Babies are beautiful. But take a look at their effect on the environment – this is not so beautiful. From day one, a child is using up resources and producing rubbish: it eats, it fills its nappy and it needs clothes, toys and books. Some couples decide not to have any children, but what about those of us who want a family? How can we raise children properly and continue to live in a way which doesn't affect the environment in a negative way?

Here's an idea – eco-parenting. It's a way to bring up a child without wasting resources. Eco-parents get their children out of nappies as early as possible, they don't give their kids a bath every single evening and they don't wash their clothes unless they are actually dirty. They also buy "green" products for their children. "We have always cared about the environment so it was obvious that we would bring up our children to respect the planet," says Marina Jack, mother of three girls. "The world would be a better place if more parents taught their children about pollution," she says.

Sometimes having a baby is what makes some people decide to go green. "He's the reason my wife and I started thinking about what we could do to protect the environment," says Richard Ross, holding his six-month old baby boy. "The most important reason to recycle is the impact it will have on our children's future," he says.

Other parents have a different opinion. "Eco-parenting is only for rich people," says Kate Milton. "I have four kids under 6 so I can't afford to buy organic food or ecologically-produced clothes. Would I buy ecological products if I had the money? No, I wouldn't. I think all this 'save the planet' stuff is just for people who want to prove how good they are."

Clearly, parents have wide-ranging opinions on eco-parenting. The debate on green upbringing is set to continue.

1 Choose the most appropriate ending(s) to complete the sentence.

1 Babies are
    A very lovely but they do use quite a lot of resources.
    B horrible.
    C pretty.

2 Some parents
  A teach their children about plants and animals.
  B help their children to live in balance with the planet.
  C don't know anything about environmental protection.

3 Marina Jack believes that other parents should
  A bring up their children in a green way.
  B not have children.
  C respect their children.

4 Some people only think about leading an eco-friendly life
  A when they don't have any children.
  B after they have children.
  C because their children ask them to.

5 Kate Milton
  A would like to buy green products.
  B doesn't have the money to buy ecological products.
  C is not interested in the eco-movement.

2 Match these statements (1–6) with the people who said them (A–F).

1 "Eco-products" are just another way for the manufacturers to make money.
2 I want him to see trees and animals and to be able to swim in clean water.
3 Turn off the light, mum.
4 Everyone knows that having children is an environmental disaster.
5 If my parents had been more careful, I wouldn't have to fight for water.
6 Our seven-year-old daughter knows all about recycling.

A A man who has decided not to have children
B Marina Jack
C Kate Milton's oldest son
D Marina Jack's daughter
E Richard Ross
F Kate Milton

3 Choose the correct alternative to complete each sentence.

1 If Joe had children he *would have taught / would teach* them about protecting the environment.
2 You *would save / would have saved* money if you bought the environmentally-friendly fridge.
3 The fair trade products *would sell / would have sold* better if they were nearer the check-out.
4 If you threw away your chemical cleaners, you *would have / would have had* more room in the cupboard.
5 She *wouldn't buy / wouldn't have bought* it if she knew how much plastic was in it.
6 If you washed your clothes less frequently, they *would last / would have lasted* longer.

Do you remember?
Conditional 2
The world would be a better place if more parents taught their children about pollution.
Would I buy ecological products if I had the money?

TEXT 3 Shopping with care

Finn is from Freiburg. At the moment he's in Brighton to improve his English. He's gone with Aidan, the boy from his host family, to visit a girl called Dee.

1 Before you listen, match what Finn says (A–F) to the pictures (1–6). Then listen and check.

A   Do you know how much water they use to produce these things? And they don't break down when people throw them away either.
B   I'm out of here.
C   Do you think this is organic? Fair trade? How can someone in England buy a mango? Don't they think about food miles here? My mum only buys local produce at the market. Think global, act local!
D   Plastic bottles, yech!
E   Don't they know in this family that the orang-utans in Borneo are dying because the west is destroying their forests to get coconut oil for their shampoo and cosmetics?
F   "These bags are biodegradable." Yeah … in a million years.

2 Choose the most appropriate ending for these sentences based on information from the text.

1   Finn and his family
  A   eat a lot of exotic fruits.
  B   think carefully about the food they buy.
  C   shop at their local supermarket.

2   According to Finn, disposable nappies
  A   are not biodegradable.
  B   break down very slowly.
  C   should not be sold in plastic packaging.

3   Finn believes that plastic bags
  A   disintegrate easily.
  B   will take a long time to break down.
  C   should be recycled.

4   Finn
  A   uses coconut shampoo but he uses a different brand.
  B   likes the fact that the shampoo is natural.
  C   is concerned about animals suffering.

5   Aidan
  A   agrees with Finn about environmental problems.
  B   would like a cool mineral water.
  C   thinks that Finn is too critical.

6   Aidan would like Finn to
  A   give his family tips about ecology.
  B   go swimming with him.
  C   stop talking about how "good" he is.

> **Everyday English**
> *to jump to conclusions*
> voreilige Schlüsse ziehen

Unit 10

3 Compare and contrast these graphs which present data about seven EU countries.

Graph 1 Percentage of the population aware of Fair Trade

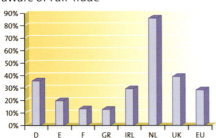

Graph 2 Percentage of the population who had bought Fair Trade goods

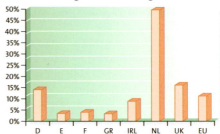

Key to abbreviations
D   Germany   F   France   IRL Ireland   UK United Kingdom
E   Spain   GR   Greece   NL   Netherlands   EU EU Average

4 **A** Aidan sees Dee in the supermarket. Listen, then do the tasks below. Some of these statements are incorrect. Correct them.

1   Aidan always does the shopping for his mum.
2   Dee has just started to do her shopping when she bumps into Aidan.
3   Some of the apples in the supermarket are covered in flies.
4   Aidan says that it doesn't matter where the bananas come from.
5   Aidan thinks it's funny that his shopping cost exactly the same as the things which Dee bought.
6   Dee's mum doesn't buy fair trade and organic products.

B **PAIR WORK** Discuss these points and then exchange ideas with another pair.

1   Describe Dee's mum's attitude to fair trade and organic products.
2   What other reasons might people have for not buying these types of goods?

5 **CLASS WORK** Choose one of the activities, A or B.

A Reducing your personal H_2O footprint
In 2008, the average daily consumption of water in Albania was 4.1 litres per person. On your own, make a rough list of how many litres of water you use on an average day. When you have your list, talk in groups about what you would have to give up to reduce your water consumption to 4.1. litres of water per day.

Optional exercise: For one day, try to restrict your consumption of water to 4.1 litres. Make notes about what you did and didn't do. Present your "low water" day to the class. Say how you felt.

B A class survey about ethical consumerism
First, brainstorm ideas about the things you buy. What do people use every day, once a week, only every so often? Then design a questionnaire to find out what makes people choose certain products. Do the survey and evaluate it.

RESULTS

Results for quiz on page 27

Mostly As and Bs = There is room for improvement.

Mostly Cs = You are a good listener.

UNIT WORD LIST

Dieses Wörterverzeichnis enthält alle Wörter in der Reihenfolge ihres Erscheinens, die nicht in der Liste des Grundwortschatzes enthalten sind, d.h. die nicht vorausgesetzt werden.

T = das Wort befindet sich in den Transcripts (Hörverständnisübungen).
coll. = umgangssprachlich

Unit 1

Page 5

Who cares? [ˌhuː ˈkeəz]	Wen kümmert's? Wer kümmert sich?	
match [mætʃ]	zuordnen	
care [keə]	Pflege, Betreuung	
care assistant [ˌkeər əˈsɪstənt]	Pfleger/in	
(the) elderly [ˈeldəli]	ältere Menschen, Senioren	
care assistant for the elderly [ˌkeər əsɪstənt fə ði ˈeldəli]	Altenpfleger/in	
counsellor [ˈkaʊnsələ]	psychologische/r Betreuer/-in	
homemaker [ˈhəʊmmeɪkə]	Hausmann/-frau	
health care assistant [ˈhelθ keər əˈsɪstənt]	Pflegeassistent/in	
nursery [ˈnɜːsəri]	Kindergarten	
nursery nurse [ˈnɜːsəri nɜːs]	Erzieher/in, Kindergärtner/in	
youth [juːθ]	Jugend	
youth worker [ˈjuːθ wɜːkə]	Jugendhelfer/in	
example [ɪgˈzɑːmpl]	Beispiel	
cook [kʊk]	Koch/Köchin	
prepare [prɪˈpeə]	(Essen:) zubereiten, kochen	

Page 6

century [ˈsentʃəri]	Jahrhundert	
planet [ˈplænɪt]	Planet	
Earth [ɜːθ]	die Erde	
plant [plɑːnt]	Pflanze	
scientist [ˈsaɪəntɪst]	(Natur-)Wissenschaftler/in	
human [ˈhjuːmən]	Mensch; menschlich	
overcrowded [ˌəʊvəˈkraʊdɪd]	überfüllt, übervölkert	
leader [ˈliːdə]	(politische/r) Führer/in	
politician [ˌpɒləˈtɪʃn]	Politiker/in	
set up [ˌset ˈʌp]	aufstellen, errichten, gründen	
invite sb [ɪnˈvaɪt]	jdn einladen	
expert [ˈekspɜːt]	Fachmann/Fachfrau, Experte/-in	
skill [skɪl]	Fähigkeit, Fertigkeit	
profession [prəˈfeʃn]	Beruf	
farmer [ˈfɑːmə]	Bauer/Bäuerin	
produce [prəˈdjuːs]	produzieren	
look after sb [lʊk ˈɑːftə]	sich um jdn kümmern	
offer [ˈɒfə]	bieten, anbieten	
nurse [nɜːs]	Krankenschwester/-pfleger	
care for sb [ˈkeə fə]	jdn pflegen, betreuen	
ill [ɪl]	krank	
reply [rɪˈplaɪ]	antworten, entgegnen	
educate [ˈedʒukeɪt]	unterrichten	
born [bɔːn]	geboren	
adult [ˈædʌlt]	Erwachsene/r	
ship [ʃɪp]	Schiff	
factory [ˈfæktəri]	Fabrik	
social worker [ˈsəʊʃl wɜːkə]	Sozialarbeiter/in	
reason [ˈriːzn]	Grund, Begründung	
be missing [bi ˈmɪsɪŋ]	fehlen	
specialist [ˈspeʃəlɪst]	Fachmann/Fachfrau, Spezialist/in	
suddenly [ˈsʌdnli]	plötzlich	
shout out [ˌʃaʊt ˈaʊt]	ausrufen	
mixture [ˈmɪkstʃə]	Mischung	
statement [ˈsteɪtmənt]	Aussage, Feststellung	
similar (to sb/sth) [ˈsɪmələ]	(jdm/einer Sache) ähnlich	
exactly [ɪgˈzæktli]	genau	
none [nʌn]	keine/r/s, niemand	
person [ˈpɜːsn]	Mensch, Person	
number [ˈnʌmbə]	Anzahl	

Page 7

discuss [dɪˈskʌs]	diskutieren	
mention [ˈmenʃn]	erwähnen	
board [bɔːd]	(Wand-)Tafel	
report to sb [rɪˈpɔːt tə]	jdm berichten	
choice [tʃɔɪs]	Wahl	
agree [əˈgriː]	zustimmen	
necessary [ˈnesəsəri]	notwendig, nötig	
sound [saʊnd]	klingen	
take place [teɪk ˈpleɪs]	stattfinden	
meeting [ˈmiːtɪŋ]	Versammlung, Sitzung, Besprechung	
meaning [ˈmiːnɪŋ]	Bedeutung	
brackets [ˈbrækɪts]	Klammern	

sentence	['sentəns]	Satz		
member	['membə]	Mitglied		
parliament	['pɑ:ləmənt]	Parlament		
Member of Parliament	[,membər əv 'pɑ:ləmənt]	Abgeordnete/r		
knowledge	['nɒlɪdʒ]	Wissen, Kenntnisse		
special knowledge	[,speʃl 'nɒlɪdʒ]	Fachwissen, Fachkenntnisse		
advice	[əd'vaɪs]	Rat, Ratschläge		
give advice	[gɪv əd'vaɪs]	(einen Rat) geben, beraten		
training	['treɪnɪŋ]	Ausbildung		
special training	[,speʃl 'treɪnɪŋ]	Fachausbildung		
caring	['keərɪŋ]	Pflege-		
ability	[ə'bɪləti]	Fähigkeit		
kind	[kaɪnd]	Art		

Page 8

trouble	['trʌbl]	Probleme, Schwierigkeiten
ice-skating	['aɪs skeɪtɪŋ]	Schlittschuhlaufen
lake	[leɪk]	See
be fun	[bi 'fʌn]	Spaß machen
interested (in)	['ɪntrəstɪd ɪn]	interessiert (an)
get interested in sth	[,get 'ɪntrəstɪd ɪn]	sich für etw interessieren
caring professions	['keərɪŋ prəfeʃnz]	Pflege-/Betreuungsberufe
army	['ɑ:mi]	Armee
ward	[wɔ:d]	Station (im Krankenhaus)
develop	[dɪ'veləp]	(sich) entwickeln
primary school	['praɪməri sku:l]	Grundschule
position	[pə'zɪʃn]	Stellung, Anstellung
usual	['ju:ʒuəl]	normal, üblich
attitude	['ætɪtju:d]	Einstellung, Haltung
single parent	[,sɪŋgl 'peərənt]	Alleinerziehende/r
mum	[mʌm]	Mutter
male	[meɪl]	männlich
role	[rəʊl]	Rolle
role model	['rəʊl mɒdl]	Vorbild
female	['fi:meɪl]	weiblich
generation	[,dʒenə'reɪʃn]	Generation
for example	[fər ɪg'zɑ:mpl]	zum Beispiel
experience	[ɪk'spɪəriəns]	(Lebens-/Berufs-)Erfahrung
physical(ly)	['fɪzɪkl]	körperlich
fit	[fɪt]	fit, in Form
mobility	[məʊ'bɪləti]	Beweglichkeit
walking aids	['wɔ:kɪŋ eɪdz]	Gehhilfe(n)
wheelchair	['wi:ltʃeə]	Rollstuhl
incontinent	[ɪn'kɒntɪnənt]	inkontinent
get sb down	[,get 'daʊn]	jdn fertig machen

Page 9

Alcoholics Anonymous	[,ælkə'hɒlɪks ə'nɒnɪməs]	Anonyme Alkoholiker
day centre	['deɪ sentə]	Tagesstätte
youth centre	['ju:θ sentə]	Jugendzentrum
drop-in	[,drɒp 'ɪn]	ohne Anmeldung
drug	[drʌg]	Droge; Medikament
addiction	[ə'dɪkʃn]	Sucht
drug addiction advice centre	[,drʌg ədɪkʃn əd'vaɪs sentə]	Drogenberatungszentrum
home for the elderly	[,həʊm fə ði 'eldəli]	Alten-/Seniorenheim
homeless	['həʊmləs]	Obdachlose/r
shelter	['ʃeltə]	Unterkunft
take turns	[teɪk 'tɜ:nz]	sich abwechseln
deal with sth	['di:l wɪð]	etw erledigen, mit etw fertig werden
park	[pɑ:k]	Park
tired	['taɪəd]	müde
childhood	['tʃaɪldhʊd]	Kindheit
shift	[ʃɪft]	Schicht
late shift	['leɪt ʃɪft]	Spätschicht
swap	[swɒp]	tauschen
scan	[skæn]	überfliegen, absuchen
summary	['sʌməri]	Zusammenfassung, Überblick
get on with sb	[,get 'ɒn wɪð]	mit jdm zurecht kommen
deal with sb	['di:l wɪð]	mit jdm zu tun haben, mit jdm umgehen
get around	[,get ə'raʊnd]	sich frei bewegen
pleasant	['pleznt]	angenehm
once	[wʌns]	einmal
quick(ly)	['kwɪk]	schnell
all the time	[,ɔ:l ðə 'taɪm]	dauernd, ständig
option	['ɒpʃn]	Möglichkeit, Option
sort	[sɔ:t]	Art, Sorte
feel low	[fi:l 'ləʊ]	niedergeschlagen sein
mean	[mi:n]	meinen
traditional	[trə'dɪʃənl]	traditionell, hergebracht

Page 10

greeting	['gri:tɪŋ]	Begrüßung
team	[ti:m]	Mannschaft
confusing	[kən'fju:zɪŋ]	verwirrend
hopefully	['həʊpfli]	hoffentlich
a couple of	[ə 'kʌpl əv]	ein paar
imagine sth	[ɪ'mædʒɪn]	sich etw vorstellen
drug addict	['drʌg ædɪkt]	Drogensüchtige/r
methadone programme	['meθədən prəʊgræm]	Methadonprogramm
confused	[kən'fju:zd]	verwirrt
worried	['wʌrid]	besorgt

whichever [wɪtʃ'evə]	egal welche/r/s	
branch [brɑːntʃ]	Zweig	
be up to sb [bi 'ʌp tə]	jds Aufgabe sein	
welcome sb ['welkəm]	jdn begrüßen, willkommen heißen	
stand [stænd]	stehen	
in front of [ɪn 'frʌnt əv]	vor	
get sth across [ˌget ə'krɒs]	etw klar machen	
phrase [freɪz]	Ausdruck	
contact ['kɒntækt]	Kontakt	
details ['diːteɪlz]	Angaben	
mobile (phone) [ˌməʊbaɪl 'fəʊn]	Handy	
Don't worry. [dəʊnt 'wʌri]	Keine Sorge.	
conversation [ˌkɒnvə'seɪʃn]	Gespräch	
registration [ˌredʒɪ'streɪʃn]	Registrierung	
form [fɔːm]	Formular	
birth [bɜːθ]	Geburt	
date of birth [ˌdeɪt əv 'bɜːθ]	Geburtsdatum	
parent ['peərənt]	Elternteil	
classmate ['klɑːsmeɪt]	Klassenkamerad/in	

Page 11

role play ['rəʊl pleɪ]	Rollenspiel
preparation [ˌprepə'reɪʃn]	Vorbereitung
magazine [ˌmægə'ziːn]	Zeitschrift
game [geɪm]	Spiel
gymnastics [dʒɪm'næstɪks]	Turnen
ready ['redi]	fertig, bereit

Page 12

client ['klaɪənt]	Patient
attract [ə'trækt]	zu etw motivieren
working conditions ['wɜːkɪŋ kəndɪʃnz]	Arbeitsbedingungen
pay [peɪ]	Bezahlung
job satisfaction ['dʒɒb sætɪsfækʃn]	Zufriedenheit im Job
career opportunities [kə'rɪər ɒpətjuːnətiz]	Aufstiegsmöglichkeiten
make a difference [ˌmeɪk ə 'dɪfrəns]	etwas bewegen
job security [ˌdʒɒb sɪ'kjʊərəti]	Arbeitsplatzsicherheit
prospects ['prɒspekts]	Aussichten
background ['bækgraʊnd]	Herkunft, Hintergrund
culture ['kʌltʃə]	Kultur
dignity ['dɪgnəti]	Würde

Unit 2

Page 13

family tree [ˌfæməli 'triː]	Stammbaum

Page 14

sociologist [ˌsəʊsi'ɒlədʒɪst]	Soziologe/-in
main [meɪn]	Haupt-
nuclear family ['njuːkliə 'fæməli]	Kernfamile
extended [ɪk'stendɪd]	erweitert
grandparents ['grænpeərənts]	Großeltern
step-parents ['steppeərənts]	Stiefeltern
step-children ['steptʃɪldrən]	Stiefkinder
migrant ['maɪgrənt]	Migrant/in, Migranten-
intercultural [ˌɪntə'kʌltʃərəl]	interkulturell
look closely [ˌlʊk 'kləʊsli]	näher betrachten
set-up ['setʌp]	*hier:* Typ, Form
fit (into sth) [fɪt]	(in etw hinein-)passen
category ['kætəgəri]	Kategorie, Klasse
behave [bɪ'heɪv]	sich verhalten
native ['neɪtɪv]	gebürtig, einheimisch, Heimat-
hold on to sth [ˌhəʊld 'ɒn tə]	an etw festhalten
tradition [trə'dɪʃn]	Tradition
home country [ˌhəʊm 'kʌntri]	Heimatland
mean [miːn]	bedeuten, heißen
unusual [ʌn'juːʒʊəl]	unüblich
marry ['mæri]	heiraten
cultural ['kʌltʃərəl]	kulturell
relationship [rɪ'leɪʃnʃɪp]	Beziehung, Verhältnis
experience [ɪk'spɪərɪəns]	erleben
belong to sb/sth [bɪ'lɒŋ tə]	jdm/zu etw gehören
reader ['riːdə]	Leser/in
comment ['kɒment]	Kommentar
type [taɪp]	etwa: in eine Schublade stecken
original(ly) [ə'rɪdʒnl]	ursprünglich
function ['fʌŋkʃn]	funktionieren
unless [ən'les]	es sei denn, außer (wenn), wenn … nicht
get in [ˌget 'ɪn]	nach Hause kommen
terrible ['terəbl]	furchtbar, fürchterlich
peace [piːs]	Frieden
quiet ['kwaɪət]	Ruhe
feeling ['fiːlɪŋ]	Gefühl
hardly ['hɑːdli]	kaum

Page 15

be around [bi ə'raʊnd]	da sein
be on one's own [bi ɒn ˌwʌnz 'əʊn]	allein sein
be lucky [bi 'lʌki]	Glück haben
argue ['ɑːgjuː]	sich streiten

compromise ['kɒmprəmaɪz]	Kompromiss	text message ['tekst mesɪdʒ]	SMS
divorced [dɪ'vɔːst]	geschieden	try on [ˌtraɪ 'ɒn]	(Kleidung etc.:) anprobieren
bring sb up [ˌbrɪŋ 'ʌp]	jdn großziehen	form [fɔːm]	bilden
biological [ˌbaɪə'lɒdʒɪkl]	biologisch	incorrect(ly) [ˌɪnkə'rekt]	falsch
case [keɪs]	Fall	correction [kə'rekʃn]	Korrektur, Verbesserung
be worried about [bi 'wʌrid əbaʊt]	sich Sorgen machen um	lonely ['ləʊnli]	einsam
		happen ['hæpən]	geschehen, passieren

Page 16

untidy [ʌn'taɪdi]	unaufgeräumt	regular(ly) ['regjələ]	regelmäßig
clean up [ˌkliːn 'ʌp]	saubermachen, aufräumen	signal word ['sɪgnəl wɜːd]	Signalwort
		simple ['sɪmpl]	einfach
mark [mɑːk]	Note	What's wrong? [ˌwɒts 'rɒŋ]	Was ist los?
homework ['həʊmwɜːk]	Hausaufgaben		
salad ['sæləd]	Salat	cry [kraɪ]	weinen, heulen, schreien
fruit [fruːt]	Obst, Früchte		
smoke [sməʊk]	rauchen	get divorced [get dɪ'vɔːst]	sich scheiden lassen
bill [bɪl]	Rechnung		
spend (money) [ˌspend 'mʌni]	(Geld) ausgeben	## Page 18	
pay well [ˌpeɪ 'wel]	(Job:) gut bezahlt sein	divorce [dɪ'vɔːs]	Scheidung
make ends meet [meɪk endz 'miːt]	über die Runden kommen	separation [ˌsepə'reɪʃn]	Trennung
		paragraph ['pærəgrɑːf]	Abschnitt, Absatz
marriage ['mærɪdʒ]	Ehe; Hochzeit	order ['ɔːdə]	Reihenfolge
guidance ['gaɪdəns]	Anleitung, Rat	emotional [ɪ'məʊʃnl]	emotional, Gefühls-
counsellor ['kaʊnsələ]	Berater/in	everyone involved [ˌevriwʌn ɪn'vɒlvd]	jede/r Beteiligte/r
marriage guidance counsellor [ˌmærɪdʒ gaɪdəns 'kaʊnsələ]	Eheberater/in	get hurt [get 'hɜːt]	verletzt werden
		immediate [ɪ'miːdiət]	unmittelbar
		financial [faɪ'nænʃl]	finanziell
mess [mes]	Chaos, Durcheinander	(child) support ['tʃaɪld səpɔːt]	Unterhalt (für ein Kind)
proper(ly) ['prɒpə]	richtig, anständig		
hang around with sb [ˌhæŋ ə'raʊnd wɪð]	herumhängen mit jdm	on top of that [ɒn 'tɒp əv ðət]	außerdem, zusätzlich
crowd [kraʊd]	Clique, Gruppe	income ['ɪnkʌm]	Einkommen
hang out with sb [ˌhæŋ 'aʊt wɪð]	mit jdm abhängen	support sb [sə'pɔːt]	Unterhalt für jdn zahlen
phase [feɪz]	Phase	twice [twaɪs]	zweimal
go through a phase [gəʊ ˌθruː ə 'feɪz]	eine Phase durchmachen	think twice about sth [ˌθɪŋk 'twaɪs əbaʊt]	sich eine Sache gut überlegen
health [helθ]	Gesundheit	split up [ˌsplɪt 'ʌp]	sich trennen
pocket money ['pɒkɪt mʌni]	Taschengeld	turn out [ˌtɜːn 'aʊt]	ausgehen
		dream [driːm]	träumen
be linked with [bi 'lɪŋkt wɪð]	in Verbindung stehen mit, zu tun haben mit	cope with sth ['kəʊp wɪð]	etw bewältigen
		betrayed [bɪ'treɪd]	verraten
behaviour [bɪ'heɪvjə]	Verhalten, Benehmen	helpless ['helpləs]	hilflos
		blame sb [bleɪm]	jdm die Schuld geben
## page 17T		go wrong [ˌgəʊ 'rɒŋ]	schieflaufen
fizzy drink ['fɪzi drɪŋk]	kohlensäurehaltigs Getränk, Brause	focus on sth ['fəʊkəs ɒn]	sich auf etw konzentrieren, sich mit etw beschäftigen
complain [kəm'pleɪn]	sich beschweren/ beklagen		
give up [ˌgɪv 'ʌp]	aufgeben	present ['preznt]	Gegenwart
		for the present [fə ðə 'preznt]	im Moment, gegenwärtig
## Page 17		use sth up [ˌjuːz 'ʌp]	etw verbrauchen
wine [waɪn]	Wein	energy ['enədʒi]	Energie
cream [kriːm]	Creme	strength [streŋθ]	Kraft

get through the time [get ˌθruː ðə ˈtaɪm]	die Zeit überstehen	marital [ˈmærɪtl]	Ehe-
get on with sth [ˌget ˈɒn wɪð]	mit etw vorankommen	area [ˈeəriə]	Gegend, Umgebung

Page 20

future [ˈfjuːtʃə]	Zukunft
aspect [ˈæspekt]	Aspekt
apart from [əˈpɑːt frəm]	abgesehen von
legal [ˈliːgl]	Rechts-, Gerichts-
move out [ˌmuːv ˈaʊt]	ausziehen
accommodation [əˌkɒməˈdeɪʃn]	Unterkunft, Bleibe
deposit [dɪˈpɒzɪt]	Kaution
landlord [ˈlændlɔːd]	Vermieter
agent [ˈeɪdʒənt]	Makler
fee [fiː]	Honorar
expenses [ɪkˈspensɪz]	Ausgaben, Aufwendungen
installation [ˌɪnstəˈleɪʃn]	Einrichtung, Installation
set sth up [ˌset ˈʌp]	etw aufbauen
item [ˈaɪtəm]	Gegenstand, Artikel, Sache
add up [ˌæd ˈʌp]	sich summieren
light bulb [ˈlaɪt bʌlb]	Glühbirne
materials [məˈtɪəriəlz]	Material
savings [ˈseɪvɪŋz]	Ersparnisse

Page 19

check [tʃek]	überprüfen, kontrollieren
appropriate [əˈprəʊpriət]	passend, zutreffend, angemessen
heading [ˈhedɪŋ]	Überschrift
provide [prəˈvaɪd]	*hier:* zahlen
bank balance [ˈbæŋk bæləns]	Kontostand
painful [ˈpeɪnfl]	schmerzhaft
involved [ɪnˈvɒlvd]	beteiligt
major [ˈmeɪdʒə]	größer, bedeutend
trauma [ˈtrɔːmə]	Trauma
psychological(ly) [ˌsaɪkəˈlɒdʒɪkl]	psychologisch
stressful [ˈstresfl]	belastend, stressig
atmosphere [ˈætməsfɪə]	Stimmung
irritable [ˈɪrɪtəbl]	gereizt
stuck in the middle *(coll.)* [ˌstʌk ɪn ðə ˈmɪdl]	*hier:* in der Mitte stehen, dazwischen stehen
betray [bɪˈtreɪ]	verraten
solution [səˈluːʃn]	Lösung
do research [ˌduː rɪˈsɜːtʃ]	recherchieren, Nachforschungen anstellen
compare [kəmˈpeə]	(miteinander) vergleichen
contrast [kənˈtrɑːst]	(einander) gegenüberstellen
couple [ˈkʌpl]	(Ehe-)Paar

stereotype [ˈsteriətaɪp]	Klischee
horrible [ˈhɒrəbl]	fürchterlich, grauenhaft, schrecklich
work [wɜːk]	*hier:* funktionieren

Unit 3

Page 21

thought [θɔːt]	Gedanke
neighbour [ˈneɪbə]	Nachbar
expect [ɪkˈspekt]	erwarten
affect [əˈfekt]	beeinträchtigen, betreffen, sich auswirken auf
grow up [ˌgrəʊ ˈʌp]	aufwachsen
danger [ˈdeɪndʒə]	Gefahr
swallow [ˈswɒləʊ]	schlucken, verschlucken
use [juːs]	Gebrauch
nutrition [njuˈtrɪʃn]	Ernährung
education [ˌedʒuˈkeɪʃn]	Bildung, Schul-, Ausbildung
lack [læk]	Mangel
violence [ˈvaɪələns]	Gewalt, Gewalttätigkeit

Page 22

report [rɪˈpɔːt]	Bericht
die [daɪ]	sterben
food [fuːd]	Essen, Nahrung
news [njuːz]	Nachrichten
• news item [ˈnjuːz aɪtəm]	Nachrichtenmeldung
hurt sb [hɜːt]	jdn verletzen, jdm weh tun
court [kɔːt]	Gericht
evidence [ˈevɪdəns]	Beweise, Beweismaterial
• give evidence [ˌgɪv ˈevɪdəns]	als Zeuge aussagen
abuse [əˈbjuːz]	missbrauchen
sexual(ly) [ˈsekʃuəl]	sexuell
tragedy [ˈtrædʒədi]	Tragödie
council [ˈkaʊnsl]	Rat, Stadtrat
service [ˈsɜːvɪs]	Dienst
department [dɪˈpɑːtmənt]	Abteilung
protection [prəˈtekʃn]	Schutz
• child protection worker [ˌtʃaɪld prəˈtekʃn wɜːkə]	Jugendamtsmitarbeiter/-in
loving [ˈlʌvɪŋ]	liebevoll
caring [ˈkeərɪŋ]	fürsorglich
neglect [nɪˈglekt]	Vernachlässigung
abuse [əˈbjuːs]	Missbrauch
child abuse [ˈtʃaɪld əbjuːs]	Kindesmissbrauch
go on [ˌgəʊ ˈɒn]	fortfahren
police [pəˈliːs]	Polizei

relative ['relətɪv]	Verwandte/r	**Page 24**	
inform [ɪn'fɔːm]	informieren	wonder ['wʌndə]	sich fragen
make the headlines [ˌmeɪk ðə 'hedlaɪnz]	in die Schlagzeilen gelangen	scared [skeəd]	verängstigt
suffer ['sʌfə]	leiden	helpline ['helplaɪn]	Notruf-Hotline
colleague ['kɒliːg]	Kollege/-in	be frightened [bi 'fraɪtnd]	Angst haben
home alone child [ˌhəʊm ə'ləʊn tʃaɪld]	Schlüsselkind	voluntary ['vɒləntri]	freiwillig, gemeinnützig
concentrate on sth ['kɒnsntreɪt ɒn]	sich auf etw konzentrieren	organization [ˌɔːgənaɪ'zeɪʃn]	Organisation
run away [ˌrʌn ə'weɪ]	weglaufen	operate ['ɒpəreɪt]	tätig sein
conditions [kən'dɪʃnz]	Bedingungen, Umstände	volunteer [ˌvɒlən'tɪə]	Freiwillige/r
		trained [treɪnd]	ausgebildet
combination [ˌkɒmbɪ'neɪʃn]	Kombination	comfort sb ['kʌmfət]	jdn trösten
tiny ['taɪni]	winzig	advise sb [əd'vaɪz]	jdn beraten
flat [flæt]	Wohnung	protect sb [prə'tekt]	jdn schützen, beschützen
uneducated [ˌʌn'edʒukeɪtɪd]	ohne/mit schlechter Ausbildung	common ['kɒmən]	(weit) verbreitet, häufig
pattern ['pætn]	Muster	bullying ['bʊliɪŋ]	Tyrannisieren, Einschüchterung, Mobbing
shocking ['ʃɒkɪŋ]	schockierend		
sort sth out [ˌsɔːt 'aʊt]	sich um etw kümmern, etw in Ordnung bringen	serious ['sɪəriəs]	ernst, schwer
		tension ['tenʃn]	Spannung
suffering ['sʌfərɪŋ]	Leid, Leiden	pregnancy ['pregnənsi]	Schwangerschaft
be worth it [bi 'wɜːθ ɪt]	es wert sein	since [sɪns]	seit
expression [ɪk'spreʃn]	Ausdruck	the mid-(19)80's [ðə ˌmɪd 'eɪtiz]	Mitte der 1980er-Jahre
title ['taɪtl]	Titel	save [seɪv]	retten
star sb [stɑː]	(Film:) mit jdm (in der Hauptrolle)	safe [seɪf]	sicher
		care for sb ['keə fə]	für jdn sorgen
actor ['æktə]	Schauspieler	spokesperson ['spəʊkspɜːsn]	Sprecher/in
although [ɔːl'ðəʊ]	obwohl	counsel ['kaʊnsl]	beraten
funny ['fʌni]	lustig, witzig	co-operate [kəʊ'ɒpəreɪt]	zusammenarbeiten, kooperieren
situation [ˌsɪtʃu'eɪʃn]	Situation, Lage		
		partnership ['pɑːtnəʃɪp]	Partnerschaft
Page 23		secondary school ['sekəndri skuːl]	weiterführende Schule
practise ['præktɪs]	üben, einüben		
definition [ˌdefɪ'nɪʃn]	Definition	successful [sək'sesfl]	erfolgreich
care [keə]	Fürsorge	expand [ɪk'spænd]	ausweiten, erweitern
attention [ə'tenʃn]	Aufmerksamkeit	area ['eəriə]	Gebiet, Bereich, Feld
unbelievable [ˌʌnbɪ'liːvəbl]	unglaublich	resource [rɪ'sɔːs]	Mittel, Hilfsmittel
		need [niːd]	Bedürfnis
pain [peɪn]	Schmerz	deaf [def]	taub
unfair [ˌʌn'feə]	ungerecht, unfair	difficulty ['dɪfɪkəlti]	Schwierigkeit
cruel [kruːəl]	brutal	group leader ['gruːp liːdə]	Gruppenleiter/in
violent ['vaɪələnt]	gewalttätig, gewaltsam	interest ['ɪntrəst]	Interesse
treatment ['triːtmənt]	Behandlung	organizer ['ɔːgənaɪzə]	Organisator/in
beat [biːt]	schlagen	part [pɑːt]	Rolle
become [bɪ'kʌm]	werden	play a part [ˌpleɪ ə 'pɑːt]	eine Rolle spielen
aged [eɪdʒd]	im Alter von	change [tʃeɪndʒ]	Veränderung
depressed [dɪ'prest]	deprimiert, depressiv	improve [ɪm'pruːv]	verbessern
doctor ['dɒktə]	Arzt/Ärztin	range [reɪndʒ]	Reihe, Palette, Auswahl
undernourishment [ˌʌndə'nʌrɪʃmənt]	Unterernährung	service ['sɜːvɪs]	Dienstleistung, Leistung
gradually ['grædʒuəli]	allmählich	opportunity [ˌɒpə'tjuːnəti]	Gelegenheit, Chance, Möglichkeit
get better [ˌget 'betə]	sich erholen, gesund werden	practical ['præktɪkl]	praktisch

encourage sb [ɪn'kʌrɪdʒ]	jdn ermutigen, ermuntern	walk into sth [ˌwɔːk 'ɪntə]	gegen etw laufen
• pupil ['pjuːpl]	Schüler/in	slam (the door) [slæm]	(die Tür) zuschlagen
support sb [sə'pɔːt]	jdn unterstützen, jdm helfen	bump into sth ['bʌmp ɪntə]	gegen etw stoßen
		• get treatment [ˌget 'triːtmənt]	sich (ärztlich etc.) behandeln lassen

Page 25

for free [fə 'friː]	umsonst, unentgeltlich
• provide [prə'vaɪd]	bieten, zur Verfügung stellen
▲ be covered in [bɪ 'kʌvəd ɪn]	übersät sein mit, voll sein von
bruise [bruːz]	blauer Fleck
face [feɪs]	Gesicht
blood [blʌd]	Blut
apply for (a job) [ə'plaɪ fə]	sich (für eine Stelle) bewerben
stairs [steəz]	Treppe
drunk [drʌŋk]	betrunken
bully sb ['bʊli]	jdn tyrannisieren, einschüchtern, mobben
join (an organization) [dʒɔɪn]	(einer Organisation) beitreten
steal [stiːl]	stehlen

Page 26

victim ['vɪktɪm]	Opfer
hit [hɪt]	schlagen
shake [ʃeɪk]	schütteln
elderly ['eldəli]	ältere/r
attack [ə'tæk]	angreifen
though [ðəʊ]	obwohl
beat sb up [ˌbiːt 'ʌp]	jdn verprügeln
point of view [ˌpɔɪnt əv 'vjuː]	Perspektive, Sicht
domestic [də'mestɪk]	häuslich
lyrics ['lɪrɪks]	Liedtext
upstairs [ˌʌp'steəz]	(im Haus:) über, oben
act [ækt]	handeln, hier: sich verhalten
proud [praʊd]	stolz
be sb's business [bɪ ˌsʌmbədiz 'bɪznəs]	jdn etwas angehen
• guess [ges]	glauben, vermuten
break [breɪk]	(zer)brechen
clumsy ['klʌmzi]	ungeschickt, linkisch
crazy ['kreɪzi]	verrückt
fight [faɪt]	Kampf, Streit; kämpfen, streiten
loud [laʊd]	laut
throw [θrəʊ]	werfen
relax [rɪ'læks]	sich entspannen, sich ausruhen
avoid [ə'vɔɪd]	vermeiden
• careful(ly) ['keəfl]	vorsichtig
quiet ['kwaɪət]	ruhig
• keep quiet [ˌkiːp 'kwaɪət]	ruhig sein

Page 27

dictionary ['dɪkʃənri]	Wörterbuch
• apologize [ə'pɒlədʒaɪz]	sich entschuldigen
• get back to sb [ˌget 'bæk tə]	sich später bei jdm melden, zurückrufen
ignore [ɪg'nɔː]	ignorieren, nicht beachten
handkerchief ['hæŋkətʃɪf]	Taschentuch
take your time [teɪk jɔː 'taɪm]	sich Zeit lassen
• continue [kən'tɪnjuː]	weitergehen
share [ʃeə]	teilen, mitteilen
repeat [rɪ'piːt]	wiederholen
• nod one's head [ˌnɒd wʌnz 'hed]	mit dem Kopf nicken
interval ['ɪntəvl]	Zeitabstand
repeat [rɪ'piːt]	wiederholen
• (the) gist [dʒɪst]	das Wesentliche, der Kern

Page 28

assess [ə'ses]	einschätzen, beurteilen, bewerten
brainstorm ['breɪnstɔːm]	Ideen sammeln
• mainly ['meɪnli]	hauptsächlich
• respond [rɪ'spɒnd]	reagieren
feedback ['fiːdbæk]	Rückmeldung
during ['djʊərɪŋ]	während
accept [ək'sept]	akzeptieren
career [kə'rɪə]	Karriere, Laufbahn
care about sb ['keər əbaʊt]	jdn mögen
• issue ['ɪʃuː]	Frage, Streitpunkt
social ['səʊʃl]	sozial
portrait ['pɔːtreɪt]	Porträt
• produce [prə'djuːs]	anfertigen
face-to-face [ˌfeɪs tə 'feɪs]	persönlich, Einzel-
run (a service) [rʌn]	(einen Dienst) betreiben
church [tʃɜːtʃ]	Kirche

Unit 4

Page 29

mental(ly) ['mentl]	geistig, Geistes-
substance ['sʌbstəns]	Substanz, Stoff, Wirkstoff
illness ['ɪlnəs]	Krankheit
alcoholism ['ælkəhɒlɪzəm]	Alkoholismus
depression [dɪ'preʃn]	Depression

flu [fluː]	Grippe	behavioural [bɪˈheɪvjərəl]	Verhaltens-
migraine [ˈmiːgreɪn]	Migräne	psychiatric [ˌsaɪkɪˈætrɪk]	psychiatrisch, psychisch
schizophrenia [ˌskɪtsəˈfriːniə]	Schizophrenie	comment [ˈkɒment]	äußern, bemerken, sagen
suffer from (an illness) [ˈsʌfə frəm]	(an einer Krankheit) leiden	be embarrassed [bi ɪmˈbærəst]	sich genieren, jdm peinlich sein
useless [ˈjuːsləs]	nutzlos, zu nichts nütze	harmless [ˈhɑːmləs]	harmlos
unhappy [ʌnˈhæpi]	unglücklich, unzufrieden	prescription [prɪˈskrɪpʃn]	Rezept, Verordnung
headache [ˈhedeɪk]	Kopfschmerz(en)	diagnose [ˈdaɪəgnəʊz]	diagnostizieren
sight [saɪt]	Sehvermögen	treat [triːt]	behandeln
patient [ˈpeɪʃnt]	Patient/in	factor [ˈfæktə]	Faktor
sick [sɪk]	schlecht, übel	concern [kənˈsɜːn]	Sorge, Beunruhigung, Anliegen
infection [ɪnˈfekʃn]	Infektion		
viral [ˈvaɪrəl]	Virus-	**Page 31**	
temperature [ˈtemprətʃə]	Fieber	worldwide [ˈwɜːldwaɪd]	weltweit
incurable [ɪnˈkjʊərəbl]	unheilbar	estimated [ˈestɪmeɪtɪd]	geschätzt
disease [dɪˈziːz]	Krankheit	dependent [dɪˈpendənt]	abhängig
contaminated [kənˈtæmɪneɪtɪd]	kontaminiert	promise [ˈprɒmɪs]	versprechen
used [juːzd]	gebraucht	overdose [ˈəʊvədəʊs]	Überdosis
needle [ˈniːdl]	Nadel	tablet [ˈtæblɪt]	Tablette
unprotected [ˌʌnprəˈtektɪd]	ungeschützt	**Page 32**	
disorder [dɪsˈɔːdə]	Störung	user [ˈjuːzə]	Benutzer/in, hier: Drogensüchtige/r
symptom [ˈsɪmptəm]	Symptom	heavy [ˈhevi]	schwer
voice [vɔɪs]	Stimme	O.D. = overdose [ˌəʊ ˈdiː, ˈəʊvədəʊs]	sich eine Überdosis setzen
hallucination [həˌluːsɪˈneɪʃn]	Halluzination	marijuana [ˌmærəˈwɑːnə]	Marihuana
destroy [dɪˈstrɔɪ]	zerstören	downer [ˈdaʊnə]	Beruhigungsmittel
damage [ˈdæmɪdʒ]	schaden, (be)schädigen, verletzen	nick [nɪk]	klauen
liver [ˈlɪvə]	Leber	stuff [stʌf]	Stoff, Zeug
cure [kjʊə]	Therapie	likely [ˈlaɪkli]	wahrscheinlich
		be scared of sb [bi ˈskeəd əv]	vor jdm Angst haben
Page 30		keep in touch with sb [ˌkiːp ɪn ˈtʌtʃ wɪð]	mit jdm in Verbindung bleiben
fact [fækt]	Fakt, Tatsache	even though [ˈiːvn ðəʊ]	obwohl
figure [ˈfɪgə]	Zahl, Ziffer	let sb down [ˌlet ˈdaʊn]	jdn im Stich lassen
be sympathetic towards sb [bi ˌsɪmpəˈθetɪk təwɔːdz]	für jdn Verständnis aufbringen	let sb get away with sth [let ˌsʌmbədi get əˈweɪ wɪð]	jdm etw durchgehen lassen, jdm etw nachsehen
mind [maɪnd]	hier: Kopf	look into sth [ˌlʊk ˈɪntə]	einer Sache nachgehen
recover [rɪˈkʌvə]	wieder gesund werden, genesen	dead [ded]	tot
completely [kəmˈpliːtli]	völlig	mate [meɪt]	Kumpel
medication [ˌmedɪˈkeɪʃn]	Medikamente	gang [gæŋ]	Clique
fit into sth [ˈfɪt ɪntə]	sich in etw einfügen	break up [ˌbreɪk ˈʌp]	sich trennen, auseinandergehen
society [səˈsaɪəti]	Gesellschaft	apprenticeship [əˈprentɪʃɪp]	Ausbildung, Lehre
isolated [ˈaɪsəleɪtɪd]	isoliert, ausgegrenzt, einsam	fancy sth [ˈfænsi]	an etw Gefallen finden
misunderstood [ˌmɪsʌndəˈstʊd]	unverstanden	guilty [ˈgɪlti]	schuldig
accept sth [əkˈsept]	etw annehmen	statistic [stəˈtɪstɪk]	hier: Zahl in einer Statistik
receive [rɪˈsiːv]	bekommen, erhalten	support group [səˈpɔːt gruːp]	Selbsthilfegruppe
medical [ˈmedɪkl]	medizinisch		
suicide [ˈsuːɪsaɪd]	Selbstmord		
commit [kəˈmɪt]	begehen		

Page 33

refer to [rɪˈfɜː tə]		sich beziehen auf
informal [ɪnˈfɔːml]		informell, umgangssprachlich
formal [ˈfɔːml]		formell, förmlich
judge [dʒʌdʒ]		Richter/in
come off [ˌkʌm ˈɒf]		absetzen, aufhören mit
tranquilizer [ˈtræŋkwəlaɪzə]		Beruhigungsmittel
extract [ˈekstrækt]		Auszug
action [ˈækʃn]		Handlung, Aktion, Maßnahme
recommend [ˌrekəˈmend]		empfehlen
suggest [səˈdʒest]		vorschlagen
local [ˈləʊkl]		örtlich, ortsansässig
GP (General Practitioner) [ˌdʒiː ˈpiː, ˌdʒenrəl prækˈtɪʃənə]		Allgemeinarzt/-ärztin, Hausarzt/-ärztin
book [bʊk]		buchen
mentoring [ˈmentɔːrɪŋ]		Betreuung, Beratung
flatmate [ˈflætmeɪt]		Mitbewohner/-in
release sb [rɪˈliːs]		jdn freilassen, (aus dem Gefängnis) entlassen
sentence [ˈsentəns]		(Gefängnis-)Strafe
serve a sentence [ˌsɜːv ə ˈsentəns]		eine Strafe verbüßen
understandably [ˌʌndəˈstændəbli]		verständlicherweise
confirm [kənˈfɜːm]		bestätigen
nausea [ˈnɔːziə]		Übelkeit
skin [skɪn]		Haut
rash [ræʃ]		Ausschlag

Page 34

countryside [ˈkʌntrisaɪd]		Land(schaft), Natur
pollution [pəˈluːʃn]		Umweltverschmutzung
dirt [dɜːt]		Dreck, Schmutz
work out [ˌwɜːk ˈaʊt]		klappen
suitable [ˈsuːtəbl]		passend
motivated [ˈməʊtɪveɪtɪd]		motiviert
make up one's mind [ˌmeɪk ˈʌp wʌnz maɪnd]		sich entscheiden

Page 35

sobriety [səˈbraɪəti]		Nüchternheit
recovery [rɪˈkʌvəri]		Genesung, Besserung
stay away from sth [ˌsteɪ əˈweɪ frəm]		sich von etw fernhalten
headteacher [ˌhedˈtiːtʃə]		(Schul-)Direktor/in
stupid [ˈstjuːpɪd]		dumm, töricht
result [rɪˈzʌlt]		Ergebnis, Resultat
attend [əˈtend]		(Schule etc.) besuchen
drop out [ˌdrɒp ˈaʊt]		(die Schule) abbrechen

rehabilitation [ˌriːəˌbɪlɪˈteɪʃn]		Rehabilitation
critic [ˈkrɪtɪk]		Kritiker/in
train sb [treɪn]		jdn ausbilden
on-site [ˌɒn ˈsaɪt]		vor Ort
therapist [ˈθerəpɪst]		Therapeut/in
criticise [ˈkrɪtɪsaɪz]		Kritik üben, kritisieren
though [ðəʊ]		allerdings, aber

Page 36

subject [ˈsʌbdʒɪkt]		(Schul-)Fach
outline [ˈaʊtlaɪn]		skizzieren
view [vjuː]		Ansicht
target group [ˈtɑːgɪt gruːp]		Zielgruppe
step [step]		Schritt
add [æd]		hinzufügen
compile [kəmˈpaɪl]		zusammenstellen
questionnaire [ˌkwestʃəˈneə]		Fragebogen
distribute [dɪˈstrɪbjuːt]		verteilen
state [steɪt]		erklären
confidential(ly) [ˌkɒnfɪˈdenʃl]		vertraulich

Unit 5

Page 37

childcare [ˈtʃaɪldkeə]		Kinderbetreuung, -fürsorge
school-age [ˈskuːl eɪdʒ]		im Schulalter, Schul-
bilingual [ˌbaɪˈlɪŋgwəl]		zweisprachig
pre- [priː]		vor-
toddler [ˈtɒdlə]		Kleinkind
mother tongue [ˈmʌðə tʌŋ]		Muttersprache
disabled [dɪsˈeɪbld]		behindert
able-bodied [ˌeɪblˈbɒdid]		nicht behindert
influence [ˈɪnfluəns]		beeinflussen
outside [ˌaʊtˈsaɪd]		draußen
artistic [ɑːˈtɪstɪk]		künstlerisch
creative(ly) [kriˈeɪtɪv]		kreativ
side [saɪd]		Seite
academic [ˌækəˈdemɪk]		akademisch
achievement [əˈtʃiːvmənt]		Leistung, Errungenschaft

Page 38

wall [wɔːl]		Wand, Mauer
sense [sens]		Sinn, Bedeutung
stick [stɪk]		Stock
leaf, leaves [liːf, liːvz]		(Laub-)Blatt, Blätter
mud [mʌd]		Schlamm
rainwater [ˈreɪn wɔːtə]		Regenwasser
not mind sth [nɒt ˈmaɪnd]		nichts gegen etw haben, nichts ausmachen

build up [ˌbɪld ˈʌp]	hier: stärken	**rod** [rɒd]	Stab
immune system [ɪˈmjuːn sɪstəm]	Immunsystem	**rug** [rʌg]	Teppich, Decke
		pillow [ˈpɪləʊ]	Kissen
as long as [əz ˈlɒŋ əz]	solange	**push sb** [pʊʃ]	jdn drängen, drängeln
waterproof [ˈwɔːtəpruːf]	wasserdicht, -fest	**goal** [gəʊl]	Ziel
dangerous [ˈdeɪndʒərəs]	gefährlich	**achieve** [əˈtʃiːv]	erreichen, erzielen, schaffen
touch [tʌtʃ]	berühren		
nowadays [ˈnaʊədeɪz]	heute, heutzutage	**certain** [ˈsɜːtn]	bestimmte/r/s
protected [prəˈtektɪd]	geschützt	**emotional(ly)** [ɪˈməʊʃənl]	emotional, gefühlsmäßig
natural [ˈnætʃrəl]	Natur-, natürlich		
paediatrician [ˌpiːdiəˈtrɪʃn]	Kinderarzt/-ärztin	**method** [ˈmeθəd]	Methode, Weise
obesity [əʊˈbiːsəti]	Fettleibigkeit	**imitation** [ˌɪmɪˈteɪʃn]	Nachahmung, Imitation
overweight [ˌəʊvəˈweɪt]	übergewichtig		
get exercise [get ˈeksəsaɪz]	Sport treiben, sich bewegen	**imagination** [ɪˌmædʒɪˈneɪʃn]	Phantasie
run about [ˌrʌn əˈbaʊt]	herumlaufen	**wonder** [ˈwʌndə]	Staunen
space [speɪs]	Raum, Platz	**community** [kəˈmjuːnəti]	Gemeinschaft, Gemeinde
frustrated [frʌˈstreɪtɪd]	frustriert		
aggression [əˈgreʃn]	Aggression	**based** [beɪst]	ansässig, basiert
relaxed [rɪˈlækst]	entspannt, locker	**non-profit** [ˌnɒnˈprɒfɪt]	gemeinnützig
confidence [ˈkɒnfɪdəns]	Selbstbewusstsein, -vertrauen	**management** [ˈmænɪdʒmənt]	Leitung, Verwaltung
flower [ˈflaʊə]	Blume, Blüte	**committee** [kəˈmɪti]	Ausschuss, Komitee
among [əˈmʌŋ]	unter, in, inmitten	**be made up of** [bi ˌmeɪd ˈʌp əv]	bestehen aus
hall [hɔːl]	Flur, Halle		
dress [dres]	sich kleiden	**staff** [stɑːf]	Personal, Angestellte
confident [ˈkɒnfɪdənt]	zuversichtlich	**dump** [dʌmp]	abladen
exist [ɪgˈzɪst]	existieren	**be involved** [bi ɪnˈvɒlvd]	einbezogen sein
lose weight [luːz ˈweɪt]	abnehmen	**make sure** [ˌmeɪk ˈʃʊə]	sicherstellen, gewährleisten
		communication [kəˌmjuːnɪˈkeɪʃn]	Kommunikation

Page 39

replace [rɪˈpleɪs]	ersetzen	**consideration for sb** [kənˌsɪdəˈreɪʃn fə]	Rücksichtnahme auf jdn
italics [ɪˈtælɪks]	Kursive, Kursivdruck		
injured [ˈɪndʒəd]	verletzt	**allow** [əˈlaʊ]	erlauben, gestatten
annoyed [əˈnɔɪd]	verärgert	**count** [kaʊnt]	zählen
link [lɪŋk]	verbinden	**according to** [əˈkɔːdɪŋ tə]	gemäß, nach, zufolge
childminder [ˈtʃaɪldmaɪndə]	Tagesmutter	**work towards sth** [ˈwɜːk təwɔːdz]	auf etw hinarbeiten
dietician [ˌdaɪəˈtɪʃn]	Ernährungsberater/in		
play [pleɪ]	Theaterstück	**set** [set]	festgesetzt
collect [kəˈlekt]	sammeln, ein-/aufsammeln	**encourage** [ɪnˈkʌrɪdʒ]	ermuntern, ermutigen
		keep apart [ˌkiːp əˈpɑːt]	auseinanderhalten
lie [laɪ]	liegen		
climb [klaɪm]	klettern	### page 41T	
strong [strɒŋ]	stark	**drop off** [ˌdrɒp ˈɒf]	hinbringen
poisonous [ˈpɔɪzənəs]	giftig	**greeting** [ˈgriːtɪŋ]	Begrüßung, Gruß
		outside [aʊtˈsaɪd]	draußen

Page 40

introduce sb/sth [ˌɪntrəˈdjuːs]	jdn/etw vorstellen	**slide** [slaɪd]	Rutsche
		sandpit [ˈsændpɪt]	Sandkasten
teaching assistant [ˈtiːtʃɪŋ əsɪstənt]	Lehrassistent/in	**painting** [ˈpeɪntɪŋ]	Gemälde
strange [streɪndʒ]	komisch	### Page 41	
educator [ˈedʒukeɪtə]	Pädadgoge/-in	**rest** [rest]	Pause, Ruhepause
mathematics [ˌmæθəˈmætɪks]	Mathematik	**creativity** [ˌkriːeɪˈtɪvəti]	Kreativität
		paint [peɪnt]	malen, bemalen
block [blɒk]	Klotz	**shy** [ʃaɪ]	schüchtern

Page 42

flyer ['flaɪə]	Broschüre, Handzettel	
balance ['bæləns]	ausgleichen, ins Gleichgewicht bringen	
pottery ['pɒtəri]	Töpfern	
clay [kleɪ]	Ton	
sculpture ['skʌlptʃə]	Bildhauerei	
be present [bi 'preznt]	anwesend sein	
selection [sɪ'lekʃn]	Auswahl	
reference book ['refərənsbʊk]	Nachschlagewerk	
workshop ['wɜːkʃɒp]	Werkstatt	
exciting [ɪk'saɪtɪŋ]	aufregend, spannend	
equipped [ɪ'kwɪpt]	ausgestattet	
construct [kən'strʌkt]	bauen, konstruieren	
model ['mɒdl]	Modell	
physics ['fɪzɪks]	Physik	
experiment [ɪk'sperɪmənt]	Experiment	
furniture ['fɜːnɪtʃə]	Möbel	
Physical Education (PE) [ˌfɪzɪkl edʒʊ'keɪʃn]	(Schul-)Sport	
weekly ['wiːkli]	wöchentlich	
be allowed to [bi ə'laʊd tə]	dürfen	
common ['kɒmən]	gemeinsam	
decision [dɪ'sɪʒn]	Entscheidung	
decision-maker [dɪ'sɪʒn meɪkə]	Entscheider, Entscheidungsträger	
summer break ['sʌmə breɪk]	Sommerferien	
take part in [teɪk 'pɑːt ɪn]	teilnehmen an	
literacy ['lɪtərəsi]	Sprachbeherrschung	

Page 43

fit sth in [ˌfɪt 'ɪn]	unterbringen
ballet class ['bæleɪ klɑːs]	Ballettkurs

Page 44

mediation [ˌmiːdi'eɪʃn]	Vermittlung, Mediation
mediate ['miːdieɪt]	vermitteln
painting ['peɪntɪŋ]	Malen
drawing ['drɔːɪŋ]	Zeichnen
session ['seʃn]	Termin, Treffen, Sitzung
pedagogical [ˌpedə'gɒdʒɪkl]	pädagogisch
swing [swɪŋ]	Schaukel
climbing frame ['klaɪmɪŋ freɪm]	Klettergerüst
unemployed [ˌʌnɪm'plɔɪd]	arbeitslos

Unit 6

Page 45

development [dɪ'veləpmənt]	Entwicklung
crayon ['kreɪən]	Wachsmalstift
get upset [get ˌʌp'set]	sich aufregen
stage [steɪdʒ]	Stadium, Phase
mirror ['mɪrə]	Spiegel
circle ['sɜːkl]	Kreis
clear(ly) ['klɪə]	klar, deutlich
smelling ['smelɪŋ]	Geruch(ssinn)
tasting ['teɪstɪŋ]	Geschmack(ssinn)
touching ['tʌtʃɪŋ]	Tastsinn
coo [kuː]	gurren
grunt [grʌnt]	grunzen, ächzen
fairy story/tale ['feəri stɔːri/teɪl]	Märchen
responsibility [rɪˌspɒnsə'bɪləti]	Verantwortung
guilt [gɪlt]	Schuld
competitive [kəm'petətɪv]	ehrgeizig, leistungsorientiert
ride [raɪd]	fahren
tricycle ['traɪsɪkl]	Dreirad
sit up [ˌsɪt 'ʌp]	sich aufsetzen
support [sə'pɔːt]	Hilfe, Unterstützung
sound [saʊnd]	Ton, Klang
cuddle sb ['kʌdl]	jdn an sich drücken
peek-a-boo [ˌpiːkə'buː]	Kuckuck-Spiel
bathroom ['bɑːθruːm]	*hier:* Toilette

Page 46

placement ['pleɪsmənt]	Praktikum
head [hed]	Leiter/in
assessment [ə'sesmənt]	Beurteilung, Bewertung
shoulder ['ʃəʊldə]	Schulter
knee [niː]	Knie
toe [təʊ]	Zehe
mouth [maʊθ]	Mund
nose [nəʊz]	Nase
brilliant ['brɪliənt]	großartig, super
complicated ['kɒmplɪkeɪtɪd]	kompliziert
bend [bend]	beugen
wave [weɪv]	winken, (mit den Armen) fuchteln
employed [ɪm'plɔɪd]	angestellt, beschäftigt

Page 47

trainee [treɪ'niː]	Auszubildende/r
foreign ['fɒrən]	ausländisch
employment [ɪm'plɔɪmənt]	Anstellung, Arbeit
sort [sɔːt]	sortieren
rhyme [raɪm]	Reim
change [tʃeɪndʒ]	*hier:* wickeln
abroad [ə'brɔːd]	im Ausland
European Union [ˌjʊərəpiːən 'juːniən]	Europäische Union
exchange programme [ɪks'tʃeɪndʒ prəʊgræm]	Austauschprogramm
qualified ['kwɒlɪfaɪd]	qualifiziert

Page 48

to begin with [tə bɪˈgɪn wɪð]	zu Beginn, am Anfang
interrupt [ˌɪntəˈrʌpt]	unterbrechen
Hang on. [ˌhæŋ ˈɒn]	Stop! Moment mal!
anyway [ˈeniweɪ]	also, jedenfalls, wie dem auch sei
energetic [ˌenəˈdʒetɪk]	anstrengend, aktiv
tired out [ˌtaɪəd ˈaʊt]	erschöpft, ausgepowert
flap (your arms about) [flæp]	(mit den Armen um sich) schlagen
connector [kəˈnektə]	Verbindungswort

Page 49

take off [ˌteɪk ˈɒf]	(Kleidung:) ausziehen
coat [kəʊt]	Jacke, Mantel
handout [ˈhændaʊt]	Arbeitsblatt
figure [ˈfɪgə]	Illustration
ankle [ˈæŋkl]	Knöchel
cheek [tʃiːk]	Wange
chin [tʃɪn]	Kinn
hip [hɪp]	Hüfte
lip [lɪp]	Lippe
neck [nek]	Hals
tooth, teeth [tuːθ, tiːθ]	Zahn, Zähne
tummy [ˈtʌmi]	Bauch

Page 50

present [ˈpreznt]	Geschenk
decoration [ˌdekəˈreɪʃn]	Dekoration, Schmuck
make decorations [meɪk ˌdekəˈreɪʃnz]	dekorieren, schmücken
chain [tʃeɪn]	Kette
paper chain [ˈpeɪpə tʃeɪn]	Girlande
instead [ɪnˈsted]	stattdessen
hang [hæŋ]	hängen, aufhängen
colourful [ˈkʌləfl]	bunt
carnival [ˈkɑːnɪvl]	Karneval
celebrate [ˈselɪbreɪt]	feiern
Chinese New Year [ˌtʃaɪˈniːz nju jɪə(r)]	Chinesisches Neujahr
go for a walk [gəʊ fər ə ˈwɔːk]	spazieren gehen
pine [paɪn]	Kiefer
cone [kəʊn]	(Kiefern-, Tannen-)Zapfen
discovery [dɪˈskʌvəri]	Entdeckung
herbs [hɜːbz]	Kräuter
smell [smel]	riechen
sparkly [ˈspɑːkli]	Glitzer-
paint [peɪnt]	Farbe
cut [kʌt]	schneiden, ausschneiden
paste [peɪst]	kleben, ein-/aufkleben
wrapping paper [ˈræpɪŋ peɪpə]	Packpapier

be based on sth [bi ˈbeɪst ɒn]	auf etw basieren, beruhen
size [saɪz]	Größe
shape [ʃeɪp]	Form
elf, elves [elf, elvz]	Elfe, Elfen
strip [strɪp]	Streifen
pin [pɪn]	(mit einer Nadel) heften, anheften
corridor [ˈkɒrɪdɔː]	Flur, Gang
bake [beɪk]	backen
recipe [ˈresəpi]	(Koch-, Back-)Rezept
Christmas [ˈkrɪsməs]	Weihnachten
seasonal [ˈsiːzənl]	Saison-
scissors [ˈsɪzəz]	Schere
glue [gluː]	Klebstoff

Page 51

unfortunately [ʌnˈfɔːtʃənətli]	leider
torn [tɔːn]	zerrissen
ingredient [ɪnˈgriːdiənt]	Zutat, Bestandteil
flour [ˈflaʊə]	Mehl
powder [ˈpaʊdə]	Pulver
sugar [ˈʃʊgə]	Zucker
chopped [tʃɒpt]	gehackt
almond [ˈɑːmənd]	Mandel
raisin [ˈreɪzn]	Rosine
grated [ˈgreɪtɪd]	gerieben
coconut [ˈkəʊkənʌt]	Kokosnuss
mashed [mæʃt]	zerdrückt
oil [ɔɪl]	einfetten
tin [tɪn]	hier: Backförmchen
pre-heat [ˌpriːˈhiːt]	vorheizen
oven [ˈʌvn]	Ofen
centigrade [ˈsentɪgreɪd]	Grad Celsius
rack [ræk]	Gitter
cool [kuːl]	abkühlen
stir [stɜː]	rühren
pour [pɔː]	gießen
mix [mɪks]	(miteinander) vermischen
spoon [spuːn]	Löffel
Easter [ˈiːstə]	Ostern
zoo [zuː]	Zoo
chicken [ˈtʃɪkɪn]	Huhn
hatch [hætʃ]	schlüpfen; ausbrüten
plastic [ˈplæstɪk]	Kunststoff, Plastik
collage [ˈkɒlɑːʒ]	Collage
rabbit [ˈræbɪt]	Kaninchen
cover [ˈkʌvə]	be-, abdecken
feather [ˈfeðə]	Feder
grass [grɑːs]	Gras
hard-boiled [ˌhɑːdˈbɔɪld]	hartgekocht
cloth [klɒθ]	Tuch

feel [fiːl]	hier: befühlen, betasten	fitted out [ˌfɪtɪd 'aʊt]	ausgestattet
colour ['kʌlə]	bemalen	tray [treɪ]	Tablett
		earn [ɜːn]	verdienen
Page 52		guesthouse ['gesthaʊs]	Pension
come up with sth [ˌkʌm 'ʌp wɪð]	(Idee etc.:) sich etw einfallen lassen, sich etw ausdenken	companion [kəm'pænɪən]	Freund/in, Gefährte/-in
		guide [gaɪd]	Führer/in
		disability [ˌdɪsə'bɪləti]	Behinderung
mood [muːd]	Stimmung	owner ['əʊnə]	Besitzer/in
tie [taɪ]	binden	relate to sth [rɪ'leɪt tə]	einen Bezug zu etw haben
shoelace ['ʃuːleɪs]	Schnürsenkel		
decorate ['dekəreɪt]	dekorieren, schmücken	network ['netwɜːk]	Netzwerk
file [faɪl]	Mappe, Ordner	independent [ˌɪndɪ'pendənt]	unabhängig
		out and about [ˌaʊt ənd ə'baʊt]	auf den Beinen, unterwegs
# Unit 7			
		rarely ['reəli]	kaum
Page 53		adjust [ə'dʒʌst]	anpassen
cerebral palsy ['serəbrəl 'pɔːlzi]	zerebrale Lähmung		
		Page 55	
blindness ['blaɪndnəs]	Blindheit	get about [ˌget ə'baʊt]	herumkommen, sich fortbewegen
deafness ['defnəs]	Taubheit		
syndrome ['sɪndrəʊm]	Syndrom	loads of ['ləʊdz əv]	eine Menge
age-related ['eɪdʒ rɪleɪtɪd]	altersbezogen, altersbedingt	get dressed [get 'drest]	sich anziehen
		parking space ['pɑːkɪŋ speɪs]	Parkplatz
aids [eɪdz]	Hilfe, Hilfsmittel		
run on sth ['rʌn ɒn]	(Fahrzeug etc.:) mit etw betrieben werden	save [seɪv]	sparen
		patient assessment manager ['peɪʃnt əsesmənt mænɪdʒə]	Patientengutachter
basket ['bɑːskɪt]	Korb		
football ground ['fʊtbɔːl graʊnd]	Fußballplatz		
		stroke [strəʊk]	Schlaganfall
		heart [hɑːt]	Herz
Page 54		heart attack ['hɑːt ətæk]	Herzanfall, Herzinfarkt
speech bubble ['spiːtʃ bʌbl]	Sprechblase	fall [fɔːl]	Sturz
		on one's own [ɒn wʌnz 'əʊn]	allein
spill [spɪl]	verschütten		
front [frʌnt]	hier: Brust	eyesight ['aɪsaɪt]	Sehvermögen
invisible [ɪn'vɪzəbl]	unsichtbar	underweight [ˌʌndə'weɪt]	untergewichtig
on a one-to-one basis [ɒn ə wʌn tə ˌwʌn 'beɪsɪs]	in Einzelsituationen	be able to [bi 'eɪbl tə]	in der Lage sein, können
		incontinence [ɪn'kɒntɪnəns]	Inkontinenz
lost [lɒst]	verloren		
eat out [ˌiːt 'aʊt]	Essen gehen	dementia [dɪ'menʃə]	Demenz
noise [nɔɪz]	Lärm	arthritis [ɑː'θraɪtɪs]	Arthritis
unwanted [ˌʌn'wɒntɪd]	ungewollt	residential care [rezɪ'denʃl 'keə]	Heimbetreuung
hearing aid ['hɪərɪŋ eɪd]	Hörgerät		
sign language ['saɪn læŋgwɪdʒ]	Gebärdensprache	nursing home ['nɜːsɪŋ həʊm]	Pflegeheim
Pull yourself together. [pʊl jɔːˌself tə'geðə]	Reiß dich zusammen		
		Page 55 T	
get fed up [get ˌfed 'ʌp]	die Nase voll haben, es satt haben	bone [bəʊn]	Knochen
		Page 56	
now and again [naʊ ənd ə'gen]	hin und wieder, ab und zu	condition [kən'dɪʃn]	Zustand, Krankheit
		healthy ['helθi]	gesund
ramp [ræmp]	Rampe	lead [liːd]	führen
lift [lɪft]	Aufzug, Fahrstuhl	value ['væljuː]	schätzen
wheel around [ˌwiːl ə'raʊnd]	(mit dem Rollstuhl) herumfahren	define [dɪ'faɪn]	definieren
		accident ['æksɪdənt]	Unfall
disabled [dɪs'eɪbld]	Behinderten-		

result [rɪˈzʌlt]	resultieren, zur Folge haben	headmaster [ˌhedˈmɑːstə]	(Schul-)Direktor
day-to-day [ˌdeɪtəˈdeɪ]	alltäglich, Alltags-	chair(person) [ˈtʃeəpɜːsn]	Vorsitzende/r, Leiter/in
set up [ˌset ˈʌp]	eingerichtet		
transport [ˈtrænspɔːt]	Verkehr, Transport		
charge (a price) [tʃɑːdʒ]	(einen Preis) berechnen		
extra [ˈekstrə]	zusätzlich		
guide dog [ˈɡaɪddɒɡ]	Blindenhund		
cab [kæb]	Taxi		
unsure [ˌʌnˈʃʊə]	unsicher		
institution [ˌɪnstɪˈtjuːʃn]	Institution, Einrichtung		
unable [ʌnˈeɪbl]	unfähig		
cause [kɔːz]	verursachen		

Page 60

passive [ˈpæsɪv]	passiv, untätig
seaside [ˈsiːsaɪd]	Küste
day trip [ˈdeɪ trɪp]	Tagesausflug
handicrafts [ˈhændɪkrɑːfts]	Handarbeiten
memory [ˈmeməri]	Gedächtnis
survey [ˈsɜːveɪ]	Überblick; Umfrage

Page 57

grid [ɡrɪd]	Gitter
normality [nɔːˈmæləti]	Normalität
bodily [ˈbɒdɪli]	körperlich
issue [ˈɪʃuː]	Problem
crutches [ˈkrʌtʃɪz]	Krücken
wheel [wiːl]	Rad
common [ˈkɒmən]	*hier:* üblich

Unit 8

Page 61

plate [pleɪt]	Teller
bean [biːn]	Bohne
bread [bred]	Brot
carrot [ˈkærət]	Möhre
nut [nʌt]	Nuss
olive [ˈɒlɪv]	Olive
oil [ɔɪl]	Öl
pineapple [ˈpaɪnæpl]	Ananas
vegetables [ˈvedʒtəblz]	Gemüse
starchy [ˈstɑːtʃi]	stärkehaltig
dairy products [ˈdeəri prɒdʌkts]	Milchprodukte
non-dairy [ˌnɒn ˈdeəri]	ohne Milchprodukte
source [sɔːs]	Quelle
protein [ˈprəʊtiːn]	Eiweiss
diet [ˈdaɪət]	Diät; Ernährung
depending on [dɪˈpendɪŋ ɒn]	abhängig von, je nach
vegetarian [ˌvedʒəˈteəriən]	Vegetarier/in

Page 58

smart [smɑːt]	schick, intelligent
individual [ˌɪndɪˈvɪdʒuəl]	einzeln
assistance [əˈsɪstəns]	Hilfe
technology [tekˈnɒlədʒi]	Technik, Technologie
remind sb [rɪˈmaɪnd]	jdn erinnern
install [ɪnˈstɔːl]	installieren, einrichten
cooker [ˈkʊkə]	Herd
record [rɪˈkɔːd]	aufnehmen
message [ˈmesɪdʒ]	Nachricht
sense [sens]	spüren
point out [ˌpɔɪnt ˈaʊt]	darauf hinweisen
consequence [ˈkɒnsɪkwəns]	Folge, Konsequenz
promote [prəˈməʊt]	fördern
safety [ˈseɪfti]	Sicherheit
firm [fɜːm]	Firma, Betrieb
set up [ˌset ˈʌp]	Aufbau
control [kənˈtrəʊl]	überwachen, kontrollieren
water tap [ˈwɔːtə tæp]	Wasserhahn
detector [dɪˈtektə]	Detektor
switch on/off [ˌswɪtʃ ˈɒn, ˈɒf]	an-/ausschalten

Page 62

balanced [ˈbælənst]	ausgewogen
calorie [ˈkæləri]	Kalorie
intake [ˈɪnteɪk]	Zufuhr, Aufnahme
rough [rʌf]	grob, ungefähr
amount [əˈmaʊnt]	Menge
level [ˈlevl]	Niveau
fluid [ˈfluːɪd]	Flüssigkeit
fresh [freʃ]	frisch
juice [dʒuːs]	Saft
contain [kənˈteɪn]	beinhalten
make up [ˌmeɪk ˈʌp]	ausmachen
liquid [ˈlɪkwɪd]	Flüssigkeit
cancer [ˈkænsə]	Krebs
western [ˈwestən]	westlich
prevent [prɪˈvent]	verhüten, verhindern
portion [ˈpɔːʃn]	Portion
cake [keɪk]	Kuchen
key [kiː]	Schlüssel
moderation [ˌmɒdəˈreɪʃn]	Mäßigung
nutritionist [njuˈtrɪʃənɪst]	Ernährungsberater/in
medicine [ˈmedsn]	Arznei, Medikament

Page 59

suffix [ˈsʌfɪks]	Endung, Endsilbe
gender [ˈdʒendə]	Geschlecht
neutral [ˈnjuːtrəl]	neutral
flight attendant [ˌflaɪt əˈtendənt]	Flugbegleiter/in
respected [rɪˈspektɪd]	respektiert, geachtet
businesswoman [ˈbɪznəswʊmən]	Geschäftsfrau

initial [ɪ'nɪʃl]	Initial	adolescent [ˌædə'lesnt]	heranwachsend, jugendlich
mass [mæs]	Masse	complication [ˌkɒmplɪ'keɪʃn]	Komplikation
weight [weɪt]	Gewicht		
height [haɪt]	Körpergröße, Höhe	hide from sth ['haɪd frəm]	sich vor etw verstecken
commonly ['kɒmənli]	allgemein	emotion [ɪ'məʊʃn]	Gefühl, Emotion
measure ['meʒə]	messen	eating habits ['iːtɪŋ hæbɪts]	Essgewohnheiten
equation [ɪ'kweɪʒn]	Gleichung		
squared [skweəd]	im Quadrat, Quadrat-	not ... either [nɒt 'aɪðə]	auch nicht
athlete ['æθliːt]	Sportler/in	compulsive [kəm'pʌlsɪv]	zwanghaft
muscle ['mʌsl]	Muskel	sufferer ['sʌfərə]	Leidende/r
tall [tɔːl]	groß (Köpergröße)	obsession [əb'seʃn]	Zwang
value ['væljuː]	Wert	crowd sb/sth out [ˌkraʊd 'aʊt]	jdn/etw verdrängen
average ['ævərɪdʒ]	Durchschnitt, durchschnittlich		
obese [əʊ'biːs]	fettleibig	socialize ['səʊʃəlaɪz]	unter Leute gehen
		bulimia [bjuː'lɪmiə]	Bulimie, Ess-Brech-Sucht

Page 63

join sth to sth [dʒɔɪn]	etw mit etw zusammenfügen, verbinden		
agree with sth [ə'griː wɪð]	mit etw übereinstimmen		

Page 65

		on the rise [ɒn ðə 'raɪz]	im Kommen
lifestyle ['laɪfstaɪl]	Lebensweise	be dying to do sth [bi 'daɪɪŋ tə]	darauf brennen etw zu tun
substitute ['sʌbstɪtjuːt]	Ersatz	warning ['wɔːnɪŋ]	Hinweis, Warnung
fight sth [faɪt]	etw bekämpfen	ideal [aɪ'diːəl]	ideal
measure ['meʒə]	Maß	meet [miːt]	(Vorbild etc.:) erreichen
combine [kəm'baɪn]	kombinieren	image ['ɪmɪdʒ]	Bild
junk [dʒʌŋk]	wörtl.: Ramsch, Mist	suit sth [suːt]	zu etw passen
raw [rɔː]	roh	fat [fæt]	dick
exchange [ɪks'tʃeɪndʒ]	tauschen, austauschen	reliable [rɪ'laɪəbl]	verlässlich
freezing ['friːzɪŋ]	eiskalt	perfect ['pɜːfɪkt]	perfekt
gap [gæp]	Lücke		
take exercise [teɪk 'eksəsaɪz]	Sport treiben		

Page 66

		allergy ['ælədʒi]	Allergie
close [kləʊs]	nah	lactose ['læktəʊz]	Laktose
calm [kɑːm]	ruhig, gelassen	intolerance [ɪn'tɒlərəns]	Intoleranz
immediately [ɪ'miːdiətli]	sofort, unverzüglich	peanuts ['piːnʌts]	Erdnüsse
		strawberry ['strɔːbəri]	Erdbeere

Page 64

eating disorder [ˌiːtɪŋ dɪs'ɔːdə]	Essstörung	hives [haɪvz]	Nesselausschlag
		itchy ['ɪtʃi]	juckend
clipping ['klɪpɪŋ]	Ausschnitt	blister ['blɪstə]	Blase
opposite ['ɒpəzɪt]	gegenüber(liegend)	digest [daɪ'dʒest]	verdauen
press conference ['pres kɒnfərəns]	Pressekonferenz	upset stomach [ˌʌpset 'stʌmək]	Magenverstimmung
dessert ['dezət]	Dessert, Süßspeise	genetic [dʒə'netɪk]	genetisch, erblich
(chocolate) bar ['tʃɒklət bɑː]	Schokoriegel	majority [mə'dʒɒrəti]	Mehrheit
		asthma ['æsmə]	Asthma
pressure ['preʃə]	Druck	attack [ə'tæk]	Anfall
become obsessed with sth [bɪˌkʌm əb'sest wɪð]	sich zwanghaft mit etw befassen	breathe [briːð]	atmen
		label ['leɪbl]	Etikett
conclusion [kən'kluːʒn]	Schluss, Schlussfolgerung	careful(ly) ['keəfəli]	sorgfältig
		hidden ['hɪdn]	verborgen
recent ['riːsnt]	aktuell	inhaler [ɪn'heɪlə]	Inhalator, Spray
study ['stʌdi]	Studie, Untersuchung		
anorexia nervosa [ˌænəˌreksiə nɜː'vəʊsə]	nervöse Magersucht		

Page 67

		enzyme ['enzaɪm]	Enzym
		lactase ['læktəz]	Laktase
anorexic [ˌænə'reksɪk]	Magersüchtige/r	allergic [ə'lɜːdʒɪk]	allergisch

reaction [ri'ækʃn]	Reaktion	limit [ˈlɪmɪt]	Grenze, Obergrenze, Limit
anti- [ˈæntaɪ]	anti-	over the limit [ˌəʊvə ðə ˈlɪmɪt]	hier: überzogen
ready to hand [ˌredi tə ˈhænd]	griffbereit	No way. [ˌnəʊ ˈweɪ]	Auf keinen Fall.
homeopathic [ˌhəʊmiəˈpæθɪk]	homöopathisch		

Page 70

de-sensitizing [ˌdiːˈsensɪtaɪzɪŋ]	Desensibilisierung
starve [stɑːv]	hungern, verhungern
berry [ˈberi]	Beere
citrus fruit [ˈsɪtrəs fruːt]	Zitrusfrucht
antibodies [ˈæntibɒdiz]	Antikörper
immune [ɪˈmjuːn]	immun
homemade [ˌhəʊmˈmeɪd]	hausgemacht
bite [baɪt]	Bissen
germ [dʒɜːm]	Keim
bacteria [bækˈtɪəriə]	Bakterien
virus [ˈvaɪrəs]	Virus
organism [ˈɔːɡənɪzəm]	Organismus
mistakenly [mɪˈsteɪkənli]	irrtümlich

Page 70 (continued)

phone network [ˈfəʊn netwɜːk]	Netzbetreiber
contract [ˈkɒntrækt]	Vertrag
mad [mæd]	verrückt
ever since [ˌevə ˈsɪns]	seitdem
debt [det]	Schuld(en)
be in debt [bi ɪn ˈdet]	Schulden haben, verschuldet sein
citizen [ˈsɪtɪzn]	Bürger/in
bureau [ˈbjʊərəʊ]	Büro
pay off [ˌpeɪ ˈɒf]	abbezahlen
instalment [ɪnˈstɔːlmənt]	Rate
influence [ˈɪnfluəns]	Einfluss
kick sb out [ˌkɪk ˈaʊt]	jdn hinauswerfen, rausschmeißen
episode [ˈepɪsəʊd]	Folge (einer Serie)
payment [ˈpeɪmənt]	Zahlung
period of time [ˈpɪəriəd əv taɪm]	Zeitspanne
run out [ˌrʌn ˈaʊt]	(Geld:) ausgehen

Page 68

blood pressure [ˈblʌd preʃə]	Blutdruck
gain [ɡeɪn]	Gewinn
No pain, no gain. [ˌnəʊ ˌpeɪn nəʊ ˈɡeɪn]	Ohne Fleiß kein Preis.
beauty [ˈbjuːti]	Schönheit
genes [dʒiːnz]	Gene
motto [ˈmɒtəʊ]	Motto
pie chart [ˈpaɪ tʃɑːt]	Tortendiagramm
preference [ˈprefrəns]	Vorlieben
likes [laɪks]	Vorlieben
dislikes [dɪsˈlaɪks]	Abneigungen
include [ɪnˈkluːd]	einschließen, aufnehmen, einbeziehen
distribute [dɪˈstrɪbjuːt]	verteilen
evaluate [ɪˈvæljueɪt]	auswerten

Page 71

reported speech [rɪˌpɔːtɪd ˈspiːtʃ]	indirekte Rede
direct speech [dəˌrekt ˈspiːtʃ]	direkte Rede
separate [ˈseprət]	sich trennen
lend [lend]	leihen, borgen
shout [ʃaʊt]	rufen, schreien, brüllen

Page 72

subject [ˈsʌbdʒɪkt]	Thema
disorderly [dɪsˈɔːdəli]	unordentlich
careers adviser [kəˈrɪəz ədvaɪzə]	Berufsberater/in
Dream on! [ˌdriːm ˈɒn]	Träum weiter!
suggestion [səˈdʒestʃən]	Vorschlag
bother with sth [ˈbɒðə wɪð]	sich um etw kümmern

Unit 9

Page 69

popular [ˈpɒpjələ]	beliebt
instant [ˈɪnstənt]	Augenblick
this instant [ðɪs ˈɪnstənt]	augenblicklich
pig [pɪɡ]	Schwein
pocket [ˈpɒkɪt]	(Hosen-, Jacken-)Tasche
shower [ˈʃaʊə]	Dusche
stink [stɪŋk]	stinken
calm down [ˌkɑːm ˈdaʊn]	sich beruhigen
filthy [ˈfɪlθi]	sehr schmutzig
pay-as-you-go [ˌpeɪ əz ju ˈɡəʊ]	Prepaid (Handy)
honest [ˈɒnɪst]	ehrlich
distract [dɪˈstrækt]	ablenken
mad (at sb) [mæd]	sauer, wütend (auf jdn)

Page 73

disappear [ˌdɪsəˈpɪə]	verschwinden
disappointed [ˌdɪsəˈpɔɪntɪd]	enttäuscht
lazy [ˈleɪzi]	faul
alternative [ɔːlˈtɜːnətɪv]	Alternative
social security [ˌsəʊʃl sɪˈkjʊərəti]	Sozialhilfe
benefits [ˈbenɪfɪts]	Leistungen

highlight ['haɪlaɪt]	hervorheben, unterstreichen		
similarity [ˌsɪmə'lærəti]	Ähnlichkeit		
suggest [sə'dʒest]	auf etw hindeuten		

Page 74

burn [bɜːn]	Verbrennung
tip [tɪp]	Tipp
refrigerator [rɪ'frɪdʒəreɪtə]	Kühlschrank
storage ['stɔːrɪdʒ]	Lagerung
tin [tɪn]	Dose
unsafe [ˌʌn'seɪf]	nicht sicher, gefährlich
scald [skɔːld]	Verbrühung
(fire)guard ['faɪəgɑːd]	Kamingitter, Kaminschirm
fire ['faɪə]	Kaminfeuer
thermostat ['θɜːməstæt]	Thermostat
tank [tæŋk]	Tank
slip [slɪp]	ausrutschen
trip [trɪp]	stolpern
loose [luːs]	lose
torn [tɔːn]	zerrissen
carpet ['kɑːpɪt]	Teppich
floor [flɔː]	Fußboden
at risk [ət 'rɪsk]	gefährdet
crime [kraɪm]	Verbrechen
statistics [stə'tɪstɪks]	Statistik(en)

Page 75

leaflet ['liːflət]	Broschüre
be aimed at [bi 'eɪmd ət]	an jdn gerichtet sein
represent [ˌreprɪ'zent]	repräsentieren
floor covering ['flɔː kʌvərɪŋ]	Fußbodenbelag
including [ɪn'kluːdɪŋ]	einschließlich
cut by half [ˌkʌt baɪ 'hɑːf]	um die Hälfte kürzen/reduzieren

Page 76

home help [ˌhəʊm 'help]	Haushaltshilfe
home shopper [ˌhəʊm 'ʃɒpə]	Einkaufshelfer/in
impatient [ɪm'peɪʃnt]	ungeduldig
stiff [stɪf]	steif
crossword puzzle ['krɒswɜːd pʌzl]	Kreuzworträtsel
serve sb [sɜːv]	jdm dienen
patient ['peɪʃnt]	geduldig
come to terms with sth [ˌkʌm tə 'tɜːmz wɪð]	sich mit etw abfinden
suppose [sə'pəʊz]	glauben
be fortunate [bi 'fɔːtʃənət]	Glück haben
love (name) ['lʌv]	(im Brief:) Liebe Grüße von (Name)
face sth [feɪs]	vor etw stehen
frustrating [frʌ'streɪtɪŋ]	frustrierend

Unit 10

Page 77

environment [ɪn'vaɪrənmənt]	Umwelt
cartoon [kɑː'tuːn]	Comic
biodegradable [ˌbaɪəʊdɪ'greɪdəbl]	biologisch abbaubar
carbon footprint [ˌkɑːbən 'fʊtprɪnt]	CO₂-Bilanz
ecological [ˌiːkə'lɒdʒɪkl]	ökologisch
ecological footprint [iːkəˌlɒdʒɪkl 'fʊtprɪnt]	Ökobilanz
trade [treɪd]	Handel
mile [maɪl]	Meile
goods [gʊdz]	Waren
decent ['diːsnt]	anständig
distance ['dɪstəns]	Entfernung
travel (a distance) ['trævl]	(eine Entfernung) zurücklegen
greenhouse ['griːnhaʊs]	Treibhaus
gas [gæs]	Gas
permanent ['pɜːmənənt]	dauerhaft, nachhaltig
damaging ['dæmɪdʒɪŋ]	schädlich
effect [ɪ'fekt]	Auswirkung, Effekt
surrounding [sə'raʊndɪŋ]	umgebend
break down [ˌbreɪk 'daʊn]	zerfallen, sich zersetzen
process ['prəʊses]	Prozess, Vorgang

Page 78

global ['gləʊbl]	global
shrink [ʃrɪŋk]	schrumpfen (lassen)
bath [bɑːθ]	Bad, Vollbad
water plants [ˌwɔːtə 'plɑːnts]	Blumen gießen
flush [flʌʃ]	(Toilette:) spülen, die Spülung betätigen
electricity [ɪˌlek'trɪsəti]	Elektrizität, Strom
drawing ['drɔːɪŋ]	Zeichnung
waste [weɪst]	vergeuden, verschwenden
plug sth in [ˌplʌg 'ɪn]	etw anschließen
power plant ['paʊə plɑːnt]	Kraftwerk
reduce [rɪ'djuːs]	reduzieren, verkleinern
power ['paʊə]	Energie, Strom
tumble drier ['tʌmbl draɪə]	Wäschetrockner
graph [grɑːf]	Diagramm
heat [hiːt]	erhitzen
pollute [pə'luːt]	verschmutzen
equipment [ɪ'kwɪpmənt]	Geräte

Page 79

government ['gʌvənmənt]	Regierung
power station ['paʊə steɪʃn]	Kraftwerk
consumer [kən'sjuːmə]	Verbraucher/in

demand [dɪˈmɑːnd]	fordern	**Page 83**	
cigarette end [ˌsɪgəˈret end]	Zigarettenkippe	**produce** [ˈprɒdjuːs]	landwirtschaftliche Erzeugnisse
dull [dʌl]	matt, stumpf	**orang-utan** [ɔːˌræŋjuːˈtæn]	Orang-Utan
consume [kənˈsjuːm]	verbrauchen	**destroy** [dɪˈstrɔɪ]	zerstören
attach [əˈtætʃ]	anbringen	**forest** [ˈfɒrɪst]	Wald
supplier [səˈplaɪə]	hier: Stromversorger	**packaging** [ˈpækɪdʒɪŋ]	Verpackung
		disintegrate [dɪsˈɪntɪgreɪt]	sich auflösen, zerfallen
		brand [brænd]	Marke

Page 80

rubbish [ˈrʌbɪʃ]	Müll
nappy [ˈnæpi]	Windel
conscious(ly) [ˈkɒnʃəs]	bewusst
raise children [ˌreɪz ˈtʃɪldrən]	Kinder großziehen
eco- [ˈiːkəʊ]	Öko-
parenting [ˈpeərəntɪŋ]	elterliche Fürsorge
be aware of sth [bi əˈweər əv]	sich einer Sache bewusst sein
respect [rɪˈspekt]	respektieren, achten
opinion [əˈpɪniən]	Meinung, Ansicht
organic [ɔːˈgænɪk]	Bio-
prove [pruːv]	beweisen
wide-ranging [ˈwaɪd reɪndʒɪŋ]	breit gefächert
debate [dɪˈbeɪt]	Debatte, Auseinandersetzung
upbringing [ˈʌpbrɪŋɪŋ]	Erziehung
be set to do sth [bi ˌset tə ˈduː]	darauf eingestellt sein etw zu tun, werden
balance [ˈbæləns]	Gleichgewicht
environmental [ɪnˌvaɪrənˈmentl]	Umwelt-

Page 81

eco-friendly [ˈiːkə frendli]	umweltfreundlich
movement [ˈmuːvmənt]	Bewegung
manufacturer [ˌmænjuˈfæktʃərə]	Hersteller, Produzent
disaster [dɪˈzɑːstə]	Katastrophe
fridge [frɪdʒ]	Kühlschrank
checkout [ˈtʃekaʊt]	Kasse
chemical [ˈkemɪkl]	chemisch
cleaner [ˈkliːnə]	Reiniger
frequently [ˈfriːkwəntli]	oft, häufig
last [lɑːst]	hier: halten

Page 82

host [həʊst]	Gastgeber/in
host family [həʊst ˈfæməli]	Gastfamilie
jump to conclusions [ˌdʒʌmp tə kənˈkluːʒnz]	voreilige Schlüsse ziehen
check sb/sth out [ˌtʃek ˈaʊt]	jdn/etw überprüfen
cool it [ˈkuːl ɪt]	sich beruhigen
Go and jump in the lake! [gəʊ ən ˌdʒʌmp ɪn ðə ˈleɪk]	Hau bloß ab!

Page 84

percentage [pəˈsentɪdʒ]	Anteil (in Prozent)
population [ˌpɒpjuˈleɪʃn]	Bevölkerung
abbreviation [əˌbriːviˈeɪʃn]	Abkürzung
bump into sb [ˈbʌmp ɪntə]	jdn zufällig treffen
fly [flaɪ]	Fliege
consumption [kənˈsʌmpʃn]	Verbrauch
optional [ˈɒpʃənl]	fakultativ
restrict [rɪˈstrɪkt]	beschränken
ethical consumerism [ˈeθɪkl kənˈsjuːmərɪzəm]	ethisches Konsumverhalten
design [dɪˈzaɪn]	entwerfen, gestalten

Page 84 T

give sb a shout (coll.) [ˌgɪv ə ˈʃaʊt]	jdm Bescheid sagen
plantation [plænˈteɪʃn]	Plantage

A-Z WORD LIST

Diese Liste enthält alle Wörter in alphabetischer Reihenfolge. Hier sind jedoch die Wörter, die zum Basic Word List (siehe S. 118) gehören, nicht aufgeführt.
Die Zahl nach dem Stichwort bezieht sich auf die Seite, auf der das Wort zum ersten Mal erscheint.
T = das Wort befindet sich in den Transcripts (Hörverständnisübungen).
coll. = umgangssprachlich

A

abbreviation Abkürzung **84**
ability Fähigkeit **7**
able: be ~ to in der Lage sein, können **55**
able-bodied nichtbehindert **37**
about: out and ~ auf den Beinen, unterwegs **54**
abroad im Ausland **47**
abuse Missbrauch, missbrauchen **22**
academic akademisch **37**
accept akzeptieren **28;**
accept sth etw annehmen **30**
accident Unfall **56**
accomodation Unterkunft, Bleibe **18**
according to gemäß, nach, zufolge **40**
achieve erreichen, erzielen, schaffen **40**
achievement Leistung, Errungenschaft **37**
act handeln, *hier:* sich verhalten **26**
action Handlung, Aktion, Maßnahme **33**
actor Schauspieler **22**
add hinzufügen **36**; **add up** sich summieren **18**
addiction Sucht **9**
adjust anpassen **54**
adolescent heranwachsend, jugendlich **64**
adult Erwachsene/r **6**
advice Rat, Ratschläge **7**; **give ~** (einen Rat) geben, beraten **7**
advise sb jdn beraten **24**
affect beeinträchtigen, betreffen, sich auswirken auf **21**
aged im Alter von **23**
agent Makler **18**
age-related altersbezogen, altersbedingt **53**
aggression Aggression **38**
agree zustimmen **7**; **agree with sth** mit etw übereinstimmen **63**
aids Hilfe, Hilfsmittel **53**
aim: be ~ed at an jdn gerichtet sein **75**
Alcoholics Anonymous Anonyme Alkoholiker **9**
alcoholism Alkoholismus **29**
all the time dauernd, ständig **9**
allergic allergisch **67**
allergy Allergie **66**
allow erlauben, gestatten **40**; **be ~ed to** dürfen **42**
almond Mandel **51**
alternative Alternative **73**
although obwohl **22**

among unter, in, inmitten **38**
amount Menge **62**
ankle Knöchel **49**
annoyed verärgert **39**
anorexia nervosa nervöse Magersucht **64**
anorexic Magersüchtige/r **64**
anti- anti- **67**
antibodies Antikörper **67**
anyway also, jedenfalls, wie dem auch sei **48**
apart from abgesehen von **18**
apologize sich entschuldigen **27**
apply for (a job) sich (für eine Stelle) bewerben **25**
apprenticeship Ausbildung, Lehre **32**
appropriate passend, zutreffend, angemessen **19**
area Gegend, Umgebung **19**; Gebiet, Bereich, Feld **24**
argue sich streiten **15**
army Armee **8**
around: be ~ da sein **15**
arthritis Arthritis **55**
artistic künstlerisch **37**
as long as solange **38**
aspect Aspekt **18**
assess einschätzen, beurteilen, bewerten **28**
assessment Beurteilung, Bewertung **46**
assistance Hilfe **58**
asthma Asthma **66**
athlete Sportler/in **62**
atmosphere Stimmung **19**
attach anbringen **79**
attack Anfall **66**; angreifen **26**
attend *(Schule etc.:)* besuchen **35**
attention Aufmerksamkeit **23**
attitude Einstellung, Haltung **8**
attract zu etw motivieren **12**
average Durchschnitt, durchschnittlich **62**
avoid vermeiden **26**
aware: be ~ of sth sich einer Sache bewusst sein **80**

B

background Herkunft, Hintergrund **12**
bacteria Bakterien **67**
bake backen **50**
balance ausgleichen, ins Gleichgewicht bringen **42**

balance Gleichgewicht **80**
balanced ausgewogen **62**
ballet class Ballettkurs **43**
bank balance Kontostand **19**
(chocolate) bar Schokoriegel **64**
based ansässig, basiert **40**; **be ~ on sth** auf etw basieren, beruhen **50**
basket Korb **53**
bath Bad, Vollbad **78**
bathroom *hier:* Toilette **45**
bean Bohne **61**
beat schlagen **23**
beat sb up jdn verprügeln **26**
beauty Schönheit **68**
become werden **23**
become obsessed with sth sich zwanghaft mit etw befassen **64**
begin: to ~ with zu Beginn, am Anfang **48**
behave sich verhalten **14**
behaviour Verhalten, Benehmen **16**
behavioural Verhaltens- **30**
belong to sb/sth jdm/zu etw gehören **14**
bend beugen **46**
benefits Leistungen **73**
berry Beere **67**
betray verraten **19**
betrayed verraten **18**
bilingual zweisprachig **37**
bill Rechnung **16**
biodegradable biologisch abbaubar **77**
biological biologisch **15**
birth Geburt **10**; **date of ~** Geburtsdatum **10**
bite Bissen **67**
blame sb jdm die Schuld geben **18**
blindness Blindheit **53**
blister Blase **66**
block Klotz **40**
blood Blut **25**; **blood pressure** Blutdruck **68**
board (Wand-)Tafel **7**
bodily körperlich **57**
bone Knochen **55T**
book buchen **33**
born geboren **6**
bother with sth sich um etw kümmern
brackets Klammern **7**
brainstorm Ideen sammeln **28**
branch Zweig **10**
brand Marke **83**
bread Brot **61**
break (zer)brechen **26**
break down zerfallen, sich zersetzen **77**
break up sich trennen, auseinandergehen **32**
breathe atmen **66**
brilliant großartig, super **46**
bring sb up jdn großziehen **15**
bruise blauer Fleck **25**
build up *hier:* stärken **38**

bulimia Bulimie, Ess-Brech-Sucht **64**
bully sb jdn tyrannisieren, einschüchtern, mobben **25**
bullying Tyrannisieren, Einschüchterung, Mobbing **24**
bump into sb jdn zufällig treffen **84**; **bump into sth** gegen etw stoßen **26**
bureau Büro **70**
burn Verbrennung **74**
business: be sb's ~ jdn etwas angehen **26**
businesswoman Geschäftsfrau **59**

C

cab Taxi **56**
cake Kuchen **62**
calm ruhig, gelassen **63**
calm down sich beruhigen **69**
calorie Kalorie **62**
cancer Krebs **62**
carbon footprint CO_2-Bilanz **77**
care Pflege, Betreuung **5**; Fürsorge **23**
care about sb jdn mögen **28**; **care for sb** jdn pflegen, betreuen **6**; für jdn sorgen **24**
care: Who ~s? Wen kümmert's? Wer kümmert sich? **5**
care assistant Pfleger/in **5**; **care assistant for the elderly** Altenpfleger/in **5**
career Karriere, Laufbahn **28**
career opportunities Aufstiegsmöglichkeiten **12**
careers adviser Berufsberater/in **72**
careful(ly) vorsichtig **26**; sorgfältig **66**
caring Pflege- **7**; fürsorglich **22**
caring professions Pflege-/Betreuungsberufe **8**
carnival Karneval **50**
carpet Teppich **74**
carrot Möhre **61**
cartoon Comic **77**
case Fall **15**
category Kategorie, Klasse **14**
cause verursachen **56**
celebrate feiern **50**
centigrade Grad Celsius **51**
century Jahrhundert **6**
cerebral palsy zerebrale Lähmung **53**
certain bestimmte/r/s **40**
chain Kette **50**
chair(person) Vorsitzende/r, Leiter/in **59**
change Veränderung **24**; *hier:* wickeln **47**
charge (a price) (einen Preis) berechnen **56**
check out überprüfen, kontrollieren **19**; **check sb/sth** jdn/etw überprüfen **82**
checkout Kasse **81**
cheek Wange **49**
chemical chemisch **81**
chicken Huhn **51**
child abuse Kindesmissbrauch **22**

child protection worker Jugendamts-
  mitarbeiter/in **22**
child support Unterhalt (für ein Kind) **18**
childcare Kinderbetreuung, -fürsorge **37**
childhood Kindheit **9**
childminder Tagesmutter **39**
chin Kinn **49**
Chinese New Year Chinesisches Neujahr **50**
choice Wahl **7**
chopped gehackt **51**
Christmas Weihnachten **50**
church Kirche **28**
cigarette end Zigarettenkippe **79**
circle Kreis **45**
citizen Bürger/in **70**
citrus fruit Zitrusfrucht **67**
classmate Klassenkamerad/in **10**
clay Ton **42**
clean up saubermachen, aufräumen **16**
cleaner Reiniger **81**
clear(ly) klar, deutlich **45**
client Patient **12**
climb klettern **39**
climbing frame Klettergerüst **44**
clipping Ausschnitt **64**
close nah **63**
cloth Tuch **51**
clumsy ungeschickt, linkisch **26**
coat Jacke, Mantel **49**
coconut Kokosnuss **51**
collage Collage **51**
colleague Kollege/-in **22**
collect sammeln, ein-/aufsammeln **39**
colour bemalen **51**
colourful bunt **50**
combination Kombination **22**
combine kombinieren **63**
come off absetzen, aufhören mit **33**
come to terms with sth sich mit etw abfinden **76**
come up with sth (Idee etc.:) sich etw einfallen
  lassen, sich etw ausdenken **52**
comfort sb jdn trösten **24**
comment Kommentar **14**; äußern, bemerken,
  sagen **30**
commit begehen **30**
committee Ausschuss, Komitee **40**
common (weit) verbreitet,
  häufig **24**; gemeinsam **42**; üblich **57**
commonly allgemein **62**
communication Kommunikation **40**
community Gemeinschaft, Gemeinde **40**
companion Freund/in, Gefährte/-in **54**
compare (miteinander) vergleichen **19**
competitive ehrgeizig, leistungsorientiert **45**
compile zusammenstellen **36**
complain sich beschweren/beklagen **17f**
completely völlig **30**

complicated kompliziert **46**
complication Komplikation **64**
compromise Kompromiss **15**
compulsive zwanghaft **64**
concentrate on sth sich auf etw konzentrieren **22**
concern Sorge, Beunruhigung, Anliegen **30**
conclusion Schluss, Schlussfolgerung **64**
condition Zustand, Krankheit **56**
conditions Bedingungen, Umstände **22**
cone (Kiefern-, Tannen-)Zapfen **50**
confidence Selbstbewusstsein, -vertrauen **38**
confident zuversichtlich **38**
confidential(ly) vertraulich **36**
confirm bestätigen **33**
confused verwirrt **10**
confusing verwirrend **10**
connector Verbindungswort **48**
conscious(ly) bewusst **80**
consequence Folge, Konsequenz **58**
consideration for sb Rücksichtnahme auf jdn **40**
construct bauen, konstruieren **42**
consume verbrauchen **79**
consumer Verbraucher/in **79**
consumerism Verbraucherbewegung,
  -herrschaft **84**
consumption Verbrauch **84**
contact Kontakt **10**
contain beinhalten **62**
contaminated kontaminiert **29**
continue weitergehen, sich fortsetzen **27**
contract Vertrag **70**
contrast (einander) gegenüberstellen **19**
control überwachen, kontrollieren **58**
conversation Gespräch **10**
coo gurren **45**
cook Koch/Köchin **5**
cooker Herd **58**
cool abkühlen **51**; **cool it** sich beruhigen **82**
co-operate zusammenarbeiten, kooperieren **24**
cope with sth etw bewältigen **18**
correction Korrektur, Verbesserung **17**
corridor Flur, Gang **50**
council Rat, Stadtrat **22**
counsel beraten **24**
counsellor psychologische/r Betreuer/in **5**;
  Berater/in **16**
count zählen **40**
countryside Land(schaft), Natur **34**
couple (Ehe-)Paar **19**; **a ~ of** ein paar **10**
court Gericht **22**
cover be-, abdecken **51**; **be ~ed in** übersät sein
  mit, voll sein von **25**
crayon Wachsmalstift **45**
crazy verrückt **26**
cream Creme **17**
creative(ly) kreativ **37**

creativity Kreativität **41**
crime Verbrechen **74**
critic Kritiker/in **35**
criticise Kritik üben, kritisieren **35**
crossword puzzle Kreuzworträtsel **76**
crowd Clique, Gruppe **16**
crowd sb/sth out jdn/etw verdrängen **64**
cruel brutal **23**
crutches Krücken **57**
cry weinen, heulen, schreien **17**
cuddle sb jdn an sich drücken **45**
cultural kulturell **14**
culture Kultur **12**
cure Therapie **29**
cut schneiden, ausschneiden **50**; **cut by half** um die Hälfte kürzen/reduzieren **75**

D

dairy products Molkereiprodukte **61**
damage schaden, (be)schädigen, verletzen **29**
damaging schädlich **77**
danger Gefahr **21**
dangerous gefährlich **38**
date of birth Geburtsdatum **10**
day centre Tagesstätte **9**
day trip Tagesausflug **60**
day-to-day alltäglich, Alltags- **56**
dead tot **32**
deaf taub **24**
deafness Taubheit **53**
deal with sb mit jdm zu tun haben, mit jdm umgehen **9**; **deal with sth** etw erledigen, mit etw fertig werden **9**
debate Debatte, Auseinandersetzung **80**
debt Schuld(en) **70**; **be in ~** Schulden haben, verschuldet sein **70**
decent anständig **77**
decision Entscheidung **42**
decision-maker Entscheider, Entscheidungsträger **42**
decorate dekorieren, schmücken **52**
decoration Dekoration, Schmuck **50**; **make ~s** dekorieren, schmücken **50**
define definieren **56**
definition Definition **23**
demand fordern **79**
dementia Demenz **55**
department Abteilung **22**
dependent abhängig **31**
depending on abhängig von, je nach **61**
deposit Kaution **18**
depressed deprimiert, depressiv **23**
depression Depression **29**
de-sensitizing Desensibilisierung **67**
dessert Dessert, Süßspeise **64**

design entwerfen, gestalten **84**
destroy zerstören **29**
details Angaben **10**
detector Detektor **58**
develop (sich) entwickeln **8**
development Entwicklung **45**
diagnose diagnostizieren **30**
dictionary Wörterbuch **27**
die sterben **22**
die: be dying to do sth darauf brennen etw zu tun **65**
diet Diät; Ernährung **61**
dietician Ernährungsberater/in **39**
difficulty Schwierigkeit **24**
digest verdauen **66**
dignity Würde **12**
direct speech direkte Rede **71**
dirt Dreck, Schmutz **34**
disability Behinderung **54**
disabled behindert **37**; **Behinderten- 54**
disappear verschwinden **73**
disappointed enttäuscht **73**
disaster Katastrophe **81**
discovery Entdeckung **50**
discuss diskutieren **7**
disease Krankheit **29**
disintegrate sich auflösen, zerfallen **83**
dislikes Abneigungen **68**
disorder Störung **29**
disorderly unordentlich
distance Entfernung **77**
distract ablenken **69**
distribute verteilen **36**
distribute verteilen **68**
divorce Scheidung **18**
divorced geschieden **15**; **get ~** sich scheiden lassen **17**
doctor Arzt/Ärztin **23**
domestic häuslich **26**
downer Beruhigungsmittel **32**
drawing Zeichnen **44**; Zeichnung **78**
dream träumen **18**
Dream on! Träum weiter! **00**
dress sich kleiden **38**; **get ~ed** sich anziehen **55**
drop off hinbringen **41T**
drop out (die Schule) abbrechen **35**
drop-in ohne Anmeldung **9**
drug Droge; Medikament **9**
drug addict Drogensüchtige/r **10**
drug addiction advice centre Drogenberatungszentrum **9**
drunk betrunken **25**
dull matt, stumpf **79**
dump abladen **40**
during während **28**

E

earn verdienen 54
Earth die Erde 6
Easter Ostern 51
eat out Essen gehen 54
eating disorder Essstörung 64
eating habits Essgewohnheiten 64
eco- Öko- 80
eco-friendly umweltfreundlich 81
ecological ökologisch 77
ecological footprint Ökobilanz 77
educate unterrichten 6
education Bildung, Schul-, Ausbildung 21
educator Pädagoge/-in 40
effect Auswirkung, Effekt 77
either: not ... ~ auch nicht 64
elderly ältere/r 26; **the elderly** ältere Menschen, Senioren 5
electricity Elektrizität, Strom 78
elf, elves Elfe, Elfen 50
embarrassed: be ~ sich genieren, jdm peinlich sein 30
emotion Gefühl, Emotion 64
emotional emotional, Gefühls- 18
emotional(ly) emotional, gefühlsmäßig 40
employed angestellt, beschäftigt 46
employment Anstellung, Arbeit 47
encourage ermuntern, ermutigen 40
encourage sb jdn ermutigen, ermuntern 24
end: make ~s meet über die Runden kommen 16
energetic anstrengend, aktiv 48
energy Energie 18
environment Umwelt 77
environmental Umwelt- 80
enzyme Enzym 67
episode Folge (einer Serie) 70
equation Gleichung 62
equipment Geräte 78
equipped ausgestattet 42
estimated geschätzt 31
ethical moralisch, ethisch 84
European Union Europäische Gemeinschaft 47
evaluate auswerten 68
even though obwohl 32
ever since seitdem 70
everyone involved jede/r Beteiligte/r 18
evidence Beweise, Beweismaterial 22; **give ~** als Zeuge aussagen 22
exactly genau 6
example Beispiel 5; **for ~** zum Beispiel 8
exchange tauschen, austauschen 63
exchange programme Austauschprogramm 47
exercise: get ~ Sport treiben, sich bewegen 38; **take ~** Sport treiben, sich bewegen 63
exciting aufregend, spannend 42
exist existieren 38

expand ausweiten, erweitern 24
expect erwarten 21
expenses Ausgaben, Aufwendungen 18
experience (Lebens-/Berufs-)Erfahrung 8; erleben 14
experiment Experiment 42
expert Fachmann/Fachfrau, Experte/-in 6
expression Ausdruck 22
extended erweitert 14
extra zusätzlich 56
extract Auszug 33
eyesight Sehvermögen 55

F

face Gesicht 25; **face-to-face** persönlich, Einzel- 28
face sth vor etw stehen 76
fact Fakt, Tatsache 30
factor Faktor 30
factory Fabrik 6
fairy story/tale Märchen 45
fall Sturz 55
family tree Stammbaum 13
fancy sth an etw Gefallen finden 32
farmer Bauer/Bäuerin 6
fat dick 65
feather Feder 51
fed up: get ~ die Nase voll haben, es satt haben 54
fee Honorar 18
feedback Rückmeldung 28
feel *hier:* befühlen, betasten 51; **feel low** niedergeschlagen sein 9
feeling Gefühl 14
female weiblich 8
fight Kampf, Streit; kämpfen, streiten 26; **fight sth** etw bekämpfen 63
figure Zahl, Ziffer 30; Illustration 49
file Mappe, Ordner 52
filthy sehr schmutzig 69
financial finanziell 18
fire Kaminfeuer 74
firm Firma, Betrieb 58
fit fit, in Form 8
fit sth in unterbringen 43; **fit into sth** in etw hineinpassen 14; sich in etw einfügen 30
fitted out ausgestattet 54
fizzy drink kohlensäurehaltigs Getränk, Brause 17T
flap (your arms about) (mit den Armen um sich) schlagen 48
flat Wohnung 22
flatmate Mitbewohner/-in 33
flight attendant Flugbegleiter/in 59
floor Fußboden 74
floor covering Fußbodenbelag 75

flour Mehl **51**
flower Blume, Blüte **38**
flu Grippe **29**
fluid Flüssigkeit **62**
flush *(Toilette:)* spülen, die Spülung betätigen **78**
fly Fliege **84**
flyer Broschüre, Handzettel **42**
focus on sth sich auf etw konzentrieren, sich mit etw beschäftigen **18**
food Essen, Nahrung **22**
football ground Fußballplatz **53**
foreign ausländisch **47**
forest Wald **83**
form Formular **10**; bilden **17**
formal formell, förmlich **33**
fortunate: be ~ Glück haben **76**
free: for ~ umsonst, unentgeltlich **25**
freezing eiskalt **63**
frequently oft, häufig **81**
fresh frisch **62**
fridge Kühlschrank **81**
frightened: be ~ Angst haben **24**
front *hier:* Brust **54**; in ~ of vor **10**
fruit Obst, Früchte **16**
frustrated frustriert **38**
frustrating frustrierend **76**
fun: be ~ Spaß machen **8**
function funktionieren **14**
funny lustig, witzig **22**
furniture Möbel **42**
future Zukunft **18**

G

gain Gewinn **68**
game Spiel **11**
gang Clique **32**
gap Lücke **63**
gas Gas **77**
gender Geschlecht **59**
generation Generation **8**
genes Gene **68**
genetic genetisch, erblich **66**
germ Keim **67**
get about herumkommen, sich fortbewegen **55**
get around sich frei bewegen **9**
get back to sb sich später bei jdm melden, zurückrufen **27**
get better sich erholen, gesund werden **23**
get divorced sich scheiden lassen **17**
get dressed sich anziehen **55**
get exercise Sport treiben, sich bewegen **38**
get fed up die Nase voll haben, es satt haben **54**
get hurt verletzt werden **18**
get in nach Hause kommen **14**
get interested in sth sich für etw interessieren **8**

get on with sb mit jdm zurecht kommen **9**; get on with sth mit etw vorankommen **18**
get sb down jdn fertig machen **8**
get sth across etw klar machen **10**
get through the time die Zeit überstehen **18**
get treatment sich (ärztlich etc.) behandeln lassen **26**
get upset sich aufregen **45**
(the) gist das Wesentliche, der Kern **27**
give advice (einen Rat) geben, beraten **7**
give evidence als Zeuge aussagen **22**
give sb a shout (coll.) jdm Bescheid geben **84T**
give up aufgeben **17T**
global global **78**
glue Klebstoff **50**
Go and jump in the lake! Hau bloß ab! **82**
go for a walk spazieren gehen **50**
go on fortfahren **22**
go through a phase eine Phase durchmachen **16**
go wrong schieflaufen **18**
goal Ziel **40**
goods Waren **77**
government Regierung **79**
GP (General Practitioner) Allgemeinarzt/-ärztin, Hausarzt/-ärztin **33**
gradually allmählich **23**
grandparents Großeltern **14**
graph Diagramm **78**
grass Gras **51**
grated gerieben **51**
greenhouse Treibhaus **77**
greeting Begrüßung **10**; Begrüßung, Gruß **41T**
grid Gitter **57**
group leader Gruppenleiter/in **24**
grow up aufwachsen **21**
grunt grunzen, ächzen **45**
(fire)guard Kamingitter, Kaminschirm **74**
guess glauben, vermuten **26**
guesthouse Pension **54**
guidance Anleitung, Rat **16**
guide Führer/in **54**
guide dog Blindenhund **56**
guilt Schuld **45**
guilty schuldig **32**
gymnastics Turnen **11**

H

hall Flur, Halle **38**
hallucination Halluzination **29**
handicrafts Handarbeiten **60**
handkerchief Taschentuch **27**
handout Arbeitsblatt **49**
hang hängen, aufhängen **50**
hang around with sb herumhängen mit jdm **16**
Hang on. Stop! Moment mal! **48**

hang out with sb mit jdm abhängen **16**
happen geschehen, passieren **17**
hard-boiled hartgekocht **51**
hardly kaum **14**
harmless harmlos **30**
hatch schlüpfen; ausbrüten **51**
head Leiter/in **46**
headache Kopfschmerz(en) **29**
heading Überschrift **19**
headline: make the ~s in die Schlagzeilen gelangen **22**
headmaster (Schul-)Direktor **59**
headteacher (Schul-)Direktor/in **35**
health Gesundheit **16**
health care assistant Pflegeassistent/in **5**
healthy gesund **56**
hearing aid Hörgerät **54**
heart Herz **55**
heart attack Herzanfall, Herzinfarkt **55**
heat erhitzen **78**
heavy schwer **32**
height Körpergröße, Höhe **62**
helpless hilflos **18**
helpline Notruf-Hotline **24**
herbs Kräuter **50**
hidden verborgen **66**
hide from sth sich vor etw verstecken **64**
highlight hervorheben, unterstreichen **73**
hip Hüfte **49**
hit schlagen **26**
hives Nesselausschlag **66**
hold on to sth an etw festhalten **14**
home alone child Schlüsselkind **22**
home country Heimatland **14**
home for the elderly Alten-/Seniorenheim **9**
home help Haushaltshilfe **76**
home shopper Einkaufshelfer/in **76**
homeless Obdachlose/r **9**
homemade hausgemacht **67**
homemaker Hausmann/-frau **5**
homeopathic homöopathisch **67**
homework Hausaufgaben **16**
honest ehrlich **69**
hopefully hoffentlich **10**
horrible fürchterlich, grauenhaft, schrecklich **20**
host Gastgeber/in **82**
host family Gastfamilie **82**
human Mensch; menschlich **6**
hurt sb jdn verletzen, jdm wehtun **22**
hurt: get ~ verletzt werden **18**

I

ice-skating Schlittschuhlaufen **8**
ideal ideal **65**
ignore ignorieren, nicht beachten **27**
ill krank **6**
illness Krankheit **29**
image Bild **65**
imagination Phantasie **40**
imagine sth sich etw vorstellen **10**
imitation Nachahmung, Imitation **40**
immediate unmittelbar **18**
immediately sofort, unverzüglich **63**
immune immun **67**
immune system Immunsystem **38**
impatient ungeduldig **76**
improve verbessern **24**
include einschließen, aufnehmen, einbeziehen **68**
including einschließlich **75**
income Einkommen **18**
incontinence Inkontinenz **55**
incontinent inkontinent **8**
incorrect(ly) falsch **17**
incurable unheilbar **29**
independent unabhängig **54**
individual einzeln **58**
infection Infektion **29**
influence Einfluss **70**; beeinflussen **37**
inform informieren **22**
informal informell, umgangssprachlich **33**
ingredient Zutat, Bestandteil **51**
inhaler Inhalator, Spray **66**
initial Initial **62**
injured verletzt **39**
install installieren, einrichten **58**
installation Einrichtung, Installation **18**
instalment Rate **70**
instant Augenblick **69**
instead stattdessen **50**
institution Institution, Einrichtung **56**
intake Zufuhr, Aufnahme **62**
intercultural interkulturell **14**
interest Interesse **24**
interested (in) interessiert (an) **8**; get ~ in sth sich für etw interessieren **8**
interrupt unterbrechen **48**
interval Zeitabstand **27**
intolerance Intoleranz **66**
introduce sb/sth jdn/etw vorstellen **40**
invisible unsichtbar **54**
invite sb jdn einladen **6**
involved beteiligt **19**; be ~ einbezogen sein **40**
irritable gereizt **19**
isolated isoliert, ausgegrenzt, einsam **30**
issue Frage, Streitpunkt **28**; Problem **57**
italics Kursive, Kursivdruck **39**
itchy juckend **66**
item Gegenstand, Artikel, Sache **18**

J

job satisfaction Zufriedenheit im Job **12**

job security Arbeitsplatzsicherheit **12**
join (an organization) (einer Organisation) beitreten **25**
join sth to sth etw mit etw zusammenfügen, verbinden **63**
judge Richter/in **33**
juice Saft **62**
jump to conclusions voreilige Schlüsse ziehen **82**
junk *wörtl.:* Ramsch, Mist **63**

K

keep apart auseinanderhalten **40**
keep in touch with sb mit jdm in Verbindung bleiben **32**
keep quiet ruhig sein **26**
key Schlüssel **62**
kick sb out jdn hinauswerfen, rausschmeißen **70**
kind Art **7**
knee Knie **46**
knowledge Wissen, Kenntnisse **7**

L

label Etikett **66**
lack Mangel **21**
lactase Laktase **67**
lactose Laktose **66**
lake See **8**; **Go and jump in the ~!** Hau bloß ab! **82**
landlord Vermieter **18**
last halten **81**
late shift Spätschicht **9**
lazy faul **73**
lead führen **56**
leader (politische/r) Führer/in **6**
leaf, leaves (Laub-)Blatt, Blätter **38**
leaflet Broschüre **75**
legal Rechts-, Gerichts- **18**
lend leihen, borgen **71**
let sb down jdn im Stich lassen **32**
let sb get away with sth jdm etw durchgehen lassen, jdn mit etw nachsehen **32**
level Niveau **62**
lie liegen **39**
lifestyle Lebensweise **63**
lift Aufzug, Fahrstuhl **54**
light bulb Glühbirne **18**
likely wahrscheinlich **32**
likes Vorlieben **68**
limit Grenze, Obergrenze, Limit **69**; **over the ~** *(Konto:)* überzogen **69**
link verbinden **39**; **be ~ed with** in Verbindung stehen mit, zu tun haben mit **16**
lip Lippe **49**
liquid Flüssigkeit **62**
literacy Sprachbeherrschung **42**

liver Leber **29**
loads of eine Menge **55**
local örtlich, ortsansässig **33**
lonely einsam **17**
look after sb sich um jdn kümmern **6**
look closely näher betrachten **14**
look into sth einer Sache nachgehen **32**
loose lose **74**
lose weight abnehmen **38**
lost verloren **54**
loud laut **26**
love (name) Liebe Grüße von (Name) **76**
loving liebevoll **22**
low: feel ~ niedergeschlagen sein **9**
lucky: be ~ Glück haben **15**
lyrics Liedtext **26**

M

mad verrückt **70**; **mad (at sb)** sauer, wütend (auf jdn) **69**
magazine Zeitschrift **11**
main Haupt- **14**
mainly hauptsächlich **28**
major größer, bedeutend **19**
majority Mehrheit **66**
make a difference etwas bewegen **12**
make decorations dekorieren, schmücken **50**
make ends meet über die Runden kommen **16**
make sure sicherstellen, gewährleisten **40**
make the headlines in die Schlagzeilen gelangen **22**
make up ausmachen **62**; **~ one's mind** sich entscheiden **34**
make up: be made up of bestehen aus **40**
male männlich **8**
management Leitung, Verwaltung **40**
manufacturer Hersteller, Produzent **81**
marijuana Marihuana **32**
marital Ehe- **19**
mark Note **16**
marriage Ehe; Hochzeit **16**
marriage guidance counsellor Eheberater/in **16**
marry heiraten **14**
mashed zerdrückt **51**
mass Masse **62**
match zuordnen **5**
mate Kumpel **32**
materials Material **18**
mathematics Mathematik **40**
mean meinen **9**; bedeuten, heißen **14**
meaning Bedeutung **7**
measure messen **62**
measure Maß **63**
mediate vermitteln **44**
mediation Vermittlung, Mediation **44**
medical medizinisch **30**

medication Medikamente **30**
medicine Arznei, Medikament **62**
meet *(Vorbild etc.:)* erreichen **65**
meeting Versammlung, Sitzung, Besprechung **7**
member Mitglied **7**
Member of Parliament Abgeordnete/r **7**
memory Gedächtnis **60**
mental(ly) geistig, Geistes- **29**
mention erwähnen **7**
mentoring Betreuung, Beratung **33**
mess Chaos, Durcheinander **16**
message Nachricht **58**
metal Metall **42**
methadone programme Methadonprogramm **10**
method Methode, Weise **40**
mid: the mid-(19)80's Mitte der 1980er-Jahre **24**
migraine Migräne **29**
migrant Migrant/in, Migranten- **14**
mile Meile **77**
mind *hier:* Kopf **30**; **make up one's ~** sich entscheiden **34**
mind: not ~ sth nichts gegen etw haben, nichts ausmachen **38**
mirror Spiegel **45**
missing: be ~ fehlen **6**
mistakenly irrtümlich **67**
misunderstood unverstanden **30**
mix (miteinander) vermischen **51**
mixture Mischung **6**
mobile (phone) Handy **10**
mobility Beweglichkeit **8**
model Modell **42**
moderation Mäßigung **62**
mood Stimmung **52**
mother tongue Muttersprache **37**
motivated motiviert **34**
motto Motto **68**
mouth Mund **46**
move out ausziehen **18**
movement Bewegung **81**
mud Schlamm **38**
mum Mutter **8**
muscle Muskel **62**

N

nappy Windel **80**
native gebürtig, einheimisch, Heimat- **14**
natural Natur-, natürlich **38**
nausea Schwindel(anfälle) **33**
necessary notwendig, nötig **7**
neck Hals **49**
need Bedürfnis **24**
needle Nadel **29**
neglect Vernachlässigung **22**
neighbour Nachbar **21**
network Netzwerk **54**

neutral neutral **59**
news Nachrichten **22**
news item Nachrichtenmeldung **22**
nick klauen **32**
No pain, no gain. Ohne Fleiß keinen Preis. **68**
No way. Auf keinen Fall. **69**
nod one's head mit dem Kopf nicken **27**
noise Lärm **54**
non-dairy ohne Milchprodukte **61**
none keine/r/s, niemand **6**
non-profit gemeinnützig **40**
normality Normalität **57**
nose Nase **46**
now and again hin und wieder; ab und zu **54**
nowadays heute, heutzutage **38**
nuclear family Kernfamilie **14**
number Anzahl **6**
nurse Krankenschwester/-pfleger **6**
nursery Kindergarten **5**
nursery nurse Erzieher/in, Kindergärtner/in **5**
nursing home Pflegeheim **55**
nut Nuss **61**
nutrition Ernährung **21**
nutritionist Ernährungsberater/in **62**

O

O.D. = overdose sich eine Überdosis setzen **32**
obese fettleibig **62**
obesity Fettleibigkeit **38**
obsession Zwang **64**
offer bieten, anbieten **6**
oil Öl **61**; einfetten **51**
olive Olive **61**
once einmal **9**
on-site vor Ort **35**
one: on a one-to-one basis in Einzelsituationen **54**
operate tätig sein **24**
opinion Meinung, Ansicht **80**
opportunity Gelegenheit, Chance, Möglichkeit **24**
opposite gegenüber(liegend) **64**
option Möglichkeit, Option **9**
optional fakultativ **84**
orang-utan Orang-Utan **83**
order Reihenfolge **18**
organic Bio- **80**
organism Organismus **67**
organization Organisation **24**
organizer Organisator/in **24**
original(ly) ursprünglich **14**
out and about auf den Beinen, unterwegs **54**
outline skizzieren **36**
outside draußen **37**
oven Ofen **51**
overcrowded überfüllt, übervölkert **6**

overdose Überdosis **31**
overweight übergewichtig **38**
own: on one's ~ allein **55**; **be on one's ~** allein sein **15**
owner Besitzer/in **54**

P

packaging Verpackung **83**
paediatrician Kinderarzt/-ärztin **38**
pain Schmerz **23**; **No ~, no gain.** Ohne Fleiß kein Preis. **68**
painful schmerzhaft **19**
paint Farbe **50**; malen, bemalen **41**
painting **41T**
paper chain Girlande **50**
paragraph Abschnitt, Absatz **18**
parent Elternteil **10**
parenting elterliche Fürsorge **80**
park Park **9**
parking space Parkplatz **55**
parliament Parlament **7**
part Rolle **24**; **play a ~** eine Rolle spielen **24**
partnership Partnerschaft **24**
passive passiv, untätig **60**
paste kleben, ein-/aufkleben **50**
patient Patient/in **29**; geduldig **76**
patient assessment manager Patientengutachter **55**
pattern Muster **22**
pay Bezahlung **12**
pay off abbezahlen **70**
pay well *(Job:)* gut bezahlt sein **16**
pay-as-you-go Prepaid *(Handy)* **69**
payment Zahlung **70**
peace Frieden **14**
peanuts Erdnüsse **66**
pedagogical pädagogisch **44**
peek-a-boo Kuckuck-Spiel **45**
percentage Anteil (in Prozent) **84**
perfect perfekt **65**
period of time Zeitspanne **70**
permanent dauerhaft, nachhaltig **77**
person Mensch, Person **6**
phase Phase **16**; **go through a ~** eine Phase durchmachen **16**
phone network Netzwerkbetreiber **70**
phrase Ausdruck **10**
Physical Education (PE) (Schul-)Sport **42**
physical(ly) körperlich **8**
physics Physik **42**
pie chart Tortendiagramm **68**
pig Schwein **69**
pillow Kissen **40**
pin (mit einer Nadel) heften, anheften **50**
pine Kiefer **50**
pineapple Ananas **61**

placement Praktikum **46**
planet Planet **6**
plant Pflanze **6**
plantation Plantage **84ᶠ**
plastic Kunststoff, Plastik **51**
plate Teller **61**
play Theaterstück **39**
play a part eine Rolle spielen **24**
pleasant angenehm **9**
plug sth in etw anschließen **78**
pocket (Hosen-, Jacken-)Tasche **69**
pocket money Taschengeld **16**
point of view Perspektive, Sicht **26**
point out darauf hinweisen **58**
poisonous giftig **39**
police Polizei **22**
politician Politiker/in **6**
pollute verschmutzen **78**
pollution Umweltverschmutzung **34**
popular beliebt **69**
population Bevölkerung **84**
portion Portion **62**
portrait Porträt **28**
position Stellung, Anstellung **8**
pottery Töpfern **42**
pour gießen **51**
powder Pulver **51**
power Energie, Strom **78**
power plant Kraftwerk **78**; **power station** Kraftwerk **79**
practical praktisch **24**
practise üben, einüben **23**
pre- vor- **37**
preference Vorlieben **68**
pregnancy Schwangerschaft **24**
pre-heat vorheizen **51**
preparation Vorbereitung **11**
prepare *(Essen:)* zubereiten, kochen **5**
prescription Rezept, Verordnung **30**
present Gegenwart **18**; Geschenk **50**; **for the ~** im Moment, gegenwärtig **18**
present: be ~ anwesend sein **42**
press conference Pressekonferenz **64**
pressure Druck **64**
prevent verhüten, verhindern **62**
primary school Grundschule **8**
process Prozess, Vorgang **77**
produce landwirtschaftliche Erzeugnisse **83**; produzieren **6**; anfertigen **28**
profession Beruf **6**
promise versprechen **31**
promote fördern **58**
proper(ly) richtig, anständig **16**
prospects Aussichten **12**
protect sb jdn schützen, beschützen **24**
protected geschützt **38**
protection Schutz **22**

protein Eiweiss **61**
proud stolz **26**
prove beweisen **80**
provide *hier:* zahlen **19**
provide bieten, zur Verfügung stellen **25**
psychiatric psychiatrisch, psychisch **30**
psychological(ly) psychologisch **19**
Pull yourself together. Reiß dich zusammen! **54**
pupil Schüler/in **24**
push sb jdn drängen, drängeln **40**

Q
qualified qualifiziert **47**
questionnaire Fragebogen **36**
quick(ly) schnell **9**
quiet Ruhe **14;** ruhig **26**

R
rabbit Kaninchen **51**
rack Gitter **51**
rainwater Regenwasser **38**
raise children Kinder großziehen **80**
raisin Rosine **51**
ramp Rampe **54**
range Reihe, Palette, Auswahl **24**
rarely kaum **54**
rash Ausschlag **33**
raw roh **63**
reaction Reaktion **67**
reader Leser/in **14**
ready fertig, bereit **11; ready to hand** griffbereit **67**
reason Grund, Begründung **6**
receive bekommen, erhalten **30**
recent aktuell **64**
recipe (Koch-, Back-)Rezept **50**
recommend empfehlen **33**
record aufnehmen **58**
recover wieder gesund werden, genesen **30**
recovery Genesung, Besserung **35**
reduce reduzieren, verkleinern **78**
refer to sich beziehen auf **33**
reference book Nachschlagewerk **42**
refrigerator Kühlschrank **74**
registration Registrierung **10**
regular(ly) regelmäßig **17**
rehabilitation Rehabilitation **35**
relate to sth einen Bezug zu etw haben **54**
relationship Beziehung, Verhältnis **14**
relative Verwandte/r **22**
relax sich entspannen, sich ausruhen **26**
relaxed entspannt, locker **38**
release sb jdn freilassen, (aus dem Gefängnis) entlassen **33**
reliable verlässlich **65**

remind sb jdn erinnern **58**
repeat wiederholen **27**
replace ersetzen **39**
reply antworten, entgegnen **6**
report Bericht **22**
report to sb jdm berichten **7**
reported speech indirekte Rede **71**
represent repräsentieren **75**
research: do ~ recherchieren, Nachforschungen anstellen **19**
residential care Heimbetreuung **55**
resource Mittel, Hilfsmittel **24**
respect respektieren, achten **80**
respected respektiert, geachtet **59**
respond reagieren **28**
responsibility Verantwortung **45**
rest Pause, Ruhepause **41**
restrict beschränken **84**
result Ergebnis, Resultat **35**
result resultieren, zur Folge haben **56**
rhyme Reim **47**
ride fahren **45**
risk: at ~ gefährdet **74**
rise: on the ~ im Kommen **65**
rod Stab **40**
role Rolle **8**
role model Vorbild **8**
role play Rollenspiel **11**
rough grob, ungefähr **62**
rubbish Müll **80**
rug Teppich, Decke **40**
run (a service) (einen Dienst) betreiben **28**
run about herumlaufen **38**
run away weglaufen **22**
run on sth *(Fahrzeug etc.:)* mit etw betrieben werden **53**
run out *(Geld:)* ausgehen **70**

S
safe sicher **24**
safety Sicherheit **58**
salad Salat **16**
sandpit Sandkasten **41T**
save retten **24;** sparen **55**
savings Ersparnisse **18**
scald Verbrühung **74**
scan überfliegen, absuchen **9**
scared verängstigt **24; be ~ of sb** vor jdm Angst haben **32**
schizophrenia Schizophrenie **29**
school-age im Schulalter, Schul- **37**
scientist (Natur-)Wissenschaftler/in **6**
scissors Schere **50**
sculpture Bildhauerei **42**
seaside Küste **60**
seasonal Saison- **50**

secondary school weiterführende Schule **24**
selection Auswahl **42**
sense Sinn, Bedeutung **38**; spüren **58**
sentence Satz **7**; (Gefängnis-)Strafe **33**
separate sich trennen **71**
separation Trennung **18**
serious ernst, schwer **24**
serve sb jdm dienen **76**
serve a sentence eine Strafe verbüßen **33**
service Dienst **22**; Dienstleistung, Leistung **24**
session Termin, Treffen, Sitzung **44**
set festgesetzt **40**; be ~ to do sth darauf eingestellt sein etw zu tun, werden **80**
set up aufstellen, errichten, gründen **6**; **set sth up** etw aufbauen **18**
set up eingerichtet **56**
set up Typ, Form **14**; Aufbau **58**
sexual(ly) sexuell **22**
shake schütteln **26**
shape Form **50**
share teilen, mitteilen **27**
shelter Unterkunft **9**
shift Schicht **9**
ship Schiff **6**
shocking schockierend **22**
shoelace Schnürsenkel **52**
shoulder Schulter **46**
shout rufen, schreien, brüllen **71**; give sb a ~ (coll.) jdm Bescheid geben **84f**
shout out ausrufen **6**
shower Dusche **69**
shrink schrumpfen (lassen) **78**
shy schüchtern **41**
sick schlecht, übel **29**
side Seite **37**
sight Sehvermögen **29**
sign language Gebärdensprache **54**
signal word Signalwort **17**
similar (to sb/sth) (jdm/einer Sache) ähnlich **6**
similarity Ähnlichkeit **73**
simple einfach **17**
since seit **24**
single parent Alleinerziehende/r **8**
sit up sich aufsetzen **45**
situation Situation, Lage **22**
size Größe **50**
skill Fähigkeit, Fertigkeit **6**
skin Haut **33**
slam (the door) (die Tür) zuschlagen **26**
slide Rutsche **41T**
slip ausrutschen **74**
smart schick, intelligent **58**
smell riechen **50**
smelling Geruch **45**
smoke rauchen **16**
sobriety Nüchternheit **35**
social sozial **28**

social security Sozialhilfe **73**
social worker Sozialarbeiter/in **6**
socialize unter Leute gehen **64**
society Gesellschaft **30**
sociologist Soziologe/-in **14**
solution Lösung **19**
sort Art, Sorte **9**; sortieren **47**
sort sth out sich um etw kümmern, etw in Ordnung bringen **22**
sound Ton, Klang **45**; klingen **7**
source Quelle **61**
space Raum, Platz **38**
sparkly Glitzer- **50**
special knowledge Fachwissen, Fachkenntnisse **7**
special training Fachausbildung **7**
specialist Fachmann/Fachfrau, Spezialist/in **6**
speech bubble Sprechblase **54**
spend (money) (Geld) ausgeben **16**
spill verschütten **54**
split up sich trennen **18**
spokesperson Sprecher/in **24**
spoon Löffel **51**
squared im Quadrat, Quadrat- **62**
staff Personal, Angestellte **40**
stage Stadium, Phase **45**
stairs Treppe **25**
stand stehen **10**
star sb (Film:) mit jdm (in der Hauptrolle) **22**
starchy stärkehaltig **61**
starve hungern, verhungern **67**
state erklären **36**
statement Aussage, Feststellung **6**
statistic hier: Zahl in einer Statistik **32**
statistics Statistik(en) **74**
stay away from sth sich von etw fernhalten **35**
steal stehlen **25**
step Schritt **36**
step-children Stiefkinder **14**
step-parents Stiefeltern **14**
stereotype Klischee **20**
stick Stock **38**
stiff steif **76**
stink stinken **69**
stir rühren **51**
storage Lagerung **74**
strange komisch **40**
strawberry Erdbeere **66**
strength Kraft **18**
stressful belastend, stressig **19**
strip Streifen **50**
stroke Schlaganfall **55**
strong stark **39**
stuck in the middle (coll.) hier: in der Mitte stehen, dazwischen stehen **19**
study Studie, Untersuchung **64**
stuff Stoff, Zeug **32**
stupid dumm, töricht **35**

subject (Schul-)Fach **36**; Thema **72**
substance Substanz, Stoff, Wirkstoff **29**
substitute Ersatz **63**
successful erfolgreich **24**
suddenly plötzlich **6**
suffer leiden **22**; **suffer from (an illness)** (an einer Krankheit) leiden **29**
sufferer Leidende/r **64**
suffering Leid, Leiden **22**
suffix Endung, Endsilbe **59**
sugar Zucker **51**
suggest vorschlagen **33**; auf etw hindeuten **73**
suggestion Vorschlag **72**
suicide Selbstmord **30**
suit sth zu etw passen **65**
suitable passend **34**
summary Zusammenfassung, Überblick **9**
summer break Sommerferien **42**
supplier *hier:* Stromversorger **79**
support Unterstützung, Hilfe **45**; Unterhalt **18**
support sb jdn unterstützen, jdm helfen **24**; Unterhalt für jdn zahlen **18**
support group Selbsthilfegruppe **32**
suppose glauben **76**
sure: make ~ sicherstellen, gewährleisten **40**
surrounding umgebend **77**
survey Überblick; Umfrage **60**
swallow schlucken, verschlucken **21**
swap tauschen **9**
swing Schaukel **44**
switch on/off an-/ausschalten **58**
sympathetic: be ~ towards sb für jdn Verständnis aufbringen **30**
symptom Symptom **29**
syndrome Syndrom **53**

T

tablet Tablette **31**
take exercise Sport treiben **63**
take off *(Kleidung:)* ausziehen **49**
take part in teilnehmen an **42**
take place stattfinden **7**
take turns sich abwechseln **9**
take your time sich Zeit lassen **27**
tall groß *(Körpergröße)* **62**
tank Tank **74**
target group Zielgruppe **36**
tasting Geschmack(ssinn) **45**
teaching assistant Lehrassistent/in **40**
team Mannschaft **10**
technology Technik, Technologie **58**
temperature Fieber **29**
tension Spannung **24**
terrible furchtbar, fürchterlich **14**
text message SMS **17**
therapist Therapeut/in **35**

thermostat Thermostat **74**
think twice about sth sich eine Sache gut überlegen **18**
this instant augenblicklich **69**
though obwohl **26**; allerdings, aber **35**
thought Gedanke **21**
throw werfen **26**
tie binden **52**
time: all the ~ dauernd, ständig **9**
tin Dose **74**; Backförmchen **51**
tiny winzig **22**
tip Tipp **74**
tired müde **9**
tired out erschöpft, ausgepowert **48**
title Titel **22**
toddler Kleinkind **37**
toe Zehe **46**
tooth, teeth Zahn, Zähne **49**
top: on ~ of that außerdem, zusätzlich **18**
torn zerrissen **51**; zerschlissen **74**
touch berühren **38**; **keep in ~ with sb** mit jdm in Verbindung bleiben **32**
touching Tastsinn **45**
trade Handel **77**
tradition Tradition **14**
traditional traditionell, hergebracht **9**
tragedy Tragödie **22**
train sb jdn ausbilden **35**
trained ausgebildet **24**
trainee Auszubildende/r **47**
training Ausbildung **7**
tranquilizer Beruhigungsmittel **33**
transport Verkehr, Transport **56**
trauma Trauma **19**
travel (a distance) (eine Entfernung) zurücklegen **77**
tray Tablett **54**
treat behandeln **30**
treatment Behandlung **23**; **get ~** sich (ärztlich etc.) behandeln lassen **26**
tricycle Dreirad **45**
trip stolpern **74**
trouble Probleme, Schwierigkeiten **8**
try on *(Kleidung etc.:)* anprobieren **17**
tumble drier Wäschetrockner **78**
tummy Bauch **49**
turn out ausgehen **18**
twice zweimal **18**
type *etwa:* in eine Schublade stecken **14**

U

unable unfähig **56**
unbelievable unglaublich **23**
undernourishment Unterernährung **23**
understandably verständlicherweise **33**
underweight untergewichtig **55**

uneducated ohne/mit schlechter Ausbildung **22**
unemployed arbeitslos **44**
unfair ungerecht, unfair **23**
unfortunately leider **51**
unhappy unglücklich, unzufrieden **29**
unless es sei denn, außer (wenn), wenn ... nicht **14**
unprotected ungeschützt **29**
unsafe nicht sicher, gefährlich **74**
unsure unsicher **56**
untidy unaufgeräumt **16**
unusual unüblich **14**
unwanted ungewollt **54**
up: be ~ to sb jds Aufgabe sein **10**
upbringing Erziehung **80**
upset: get ~ sich aufregen **45**
upset stomach Magenverstimmung **66**
upstairs *(im Haus:)* über, oben **26**
use Gebrauch **21**
use sth up etw verbrauchen **18**
used gebraucht **29**
useless nutzlos, zu nichts nütze **29**
user Benutzer/in, *hier:* Drogensüchtige/r **32**
usual normal, üblich **8**

V

value schätzen **56**
value Wert **62**
vegetables Gemüse **61**
vegetarian Vegetarier/in **61**
victim Opfer **26**
view Ansicht **36**
violence Gewalt, Gewalttätigkeit **21**
violent gewalttätig, gewaltsam **23**
viral Virus- **29**
virus Virus **67**
voice Stimme **29**
voluntary freiwillig, gemeinnützig **24**
volunteer Freiwillige/r **24**

W

walk: go for a ~ spazieren gehen **50**
walk into sth gegen etw laufen **26**
walking aid(s) Gehhilfe(n) **8**
wall Wand, Mauer **38**
ward Station (im Krankenhaus) **8**
warning Hinweis, Warnung **65**
waste vergeuden, verschwenden **78**
water plants Blumen gießen **78**
water tap Wasserhahn **58**
waterproof wasserdicht, -fest **38**
wave winken, (mit den Armen) fuchteln **46**
way: No ~. Auf keinen Fall. **69**
weekly wöchentlich **42**

weight Gewicht **62**; **lose ~** abnehmen **38**
welcome sb jdn begrüßen, willkommen heißen **10**
western westlich **62**
wheel Rad **57**
wheel around (mit dem Rollstuhl) herumfahren **54**
wheelchair Rollstuhl **8**
whichever egal welche/r/s **10**
wide-ranging breit gefächert **80**
wine Wein **17**
wonder sich fragen **24**
wonder Staunen **40**
work *hier:* funktionieren **20**
work out klappen **34**
work towards sth auf etw hinarbeiten **40**
working conditions Arbeitsbedingungen **12**
workshop Werkstatt **42**
worldwide weltweit **31**
worried besorgt **10**; **be ~ about** sich Sorgen machen um **15**
worry: Don't ~. Keine Sorge. **10**
worth: be ~ it es wert sein **22**
wrapping paper Packpapier **50**
wrong: go ~ schieflaufen **18**; **What's ~?** Was ist los? **17**

Y

youth Jugend **5**
youth centre Jugendzentrum **9**
youth worker Jugendhelfer/in **5**

Z

zoo Zoo **51**

BASIC WORD LIST

Diese Liste enthält ca. 600 Grundwörter, die in **Baustein Soziales** als bekannt vorausgesetzt werden. Nicht aufgeführt, jedoch vorausgesetzt sind internationale Wörter (taxi, email usw.) und einige sehr elementare Wörter wie Pronomen, Zahlen und Tage.

A

a lot (of) viel, sehr
above über, oben
actual(ly) tatsächlich
afternoon Nachmittag
afterwards danach
again wieder
against gegen
age Zeitalter, Alter
air Luft
airport Flughafen
almost fast, beinahe
already schon, bereits
always immer
American amerikanisch
angry wütend, verärgert
animal Tier
another noch eine
answer Antwort, Lösung; (be)antworten
anybody jemand, jede/r
anyone jemand, jede/r
anything etwas, alles
around herum
arrive ankommen
ask fragen, bitten
at home zu Hause, daheim
Australian australisch
autumn Herbst
available verfügbar
away weg, entfernt

B

back zurück
bad schlecht, schlimm
bag Tasche, Beutel
baker Bäcker/in
bakery Bäckerei
be sein
beautiful schön
because weil
bed Bett
bedroom Schlafzimmer
before vor(her)
begin anfangen, beginnen
beginning Anfang
believe glauben
belong gehören
below unter, unten

best beste/r/s, am besten
better besser
between zwischen
big groß
bike Rad
biker (Motor-)Radfahrer/in
biography Biographie
birthday Geburtstag
bit (ein) bisschen
blue blau
body Körper
book Buch; buchen, bestellen
bored gelangweilt
boring langweilig
both beide
bottle Flasche
box Kasten, Kästchen, Schachtel
boyfriend Freund
break Pause; brechen
breakfast Frühstück
bring bringen, holen
brother Bruder
brown braun
building Gebäude
bus (Linien-)Bus
business Geschäft, Firma
busy beschäftigt, besetzt
buy kaufen
by durch, mit, bei

C

cake Kuchen, Torte
be called heißen
caller Anrufer/in
can dürfen, können
car Auto
card Karte
careful vorsichtig, sorgfältig
cat Katze
centre Zentrum
change (Ver-)Änderung; (aus)wechseln, (sich) ändern
character Charakter
chat Unterhaltung; sich unterhalten
chatroom Chatroom, Gesprächsrunde
cheese Käse

child Kind
children Kinder
choose (aus)wählen
Christmas Weihnachten
church Kirche
cigarette Zigarette
city (Groß-)Stadt
class Klasse
classmate Klassenkamerad/-in
clean reinigen, säubern; sauber
climb klettern, (ein)steigen
clock Uhr
close schließen
close (to) nahe
clothes Kleidung, Kleider
coffee Kaffee
cold kalt
collect sammeln
college Fachhochschule
colour Farbe
come kommen
comedy Komödie
complain sich beklagen, (sich) beschweren, reklamieren
complete vollständig; vervollständigen
continent Erdteil, Kontinent
continue fortfahren, fortsetzen
cook kochen; Koch, Köchin
copy Kopie; kopieren
cost Kosten; kosten
country Land, Staat
course Kurs, Lehrgang, Gang
crazy verrückt
cup Tasse
cut schneiden

D

dance tanzen; Tanz
dancer Tänzer/in
danger Gefahr
dangerous gefährlich
dark Dunkelheit; dunkel
daughter Tochter
day Tag
dead tot
death Tod

decide (sich) entscheiden, beschließen
describe beschreiben
description Beschreibung, Schilderung
desk (Schreib-)Tisch
diagram Diagramm, Abbildung
die sterben
diet Diät
difference Unterschied
different anders, verschieden
difficult schwer, schwierig
dinner (Abend-)Essen
dislike nicht mögen
do tun, machen
document Dokument, Papier
dog Hund
door Tür
double doppelt
down unten, hinunter
drawing Zeichnung
dream Traum; träumen
drink Getränk; trinken
drive (Auto) fahren
drug Droge
dry trocken; trocknen

E
each jede/r/s
ear Ohr
early früh
east Osten
Easter Ostern
easy leicht, einfach
eat essen
either entweder
end Ende, Schluss; (be)enden
ending Ende
English-speaking englischsprachig
enjoy genießen, gefallen
enough ausreichend, genug
even sogar (noch)
evening Abend
ever je(mals)
every jede/r/s
everybody jede/r
everyone jede/r/s, alle
everything alles
everywhere überall
exam Examen
exercise Übung
expensive teuer
explain erklären
expression Ausdruck
eye Auge

F
factory Fabrik
fall fallen
false falsch
family Familie
famous berühmt
fan Fan, Anhänger/in
far weit (entfernt)
farm Bauernhof
farmer Bauer, Bäuerin
fast schnell
fast food Schnellimbiss
fat fett
favourite Lieblings-
feel (sich) fühlen
female weiblich, Frauen
few ein paar, wenig/e
fight (be)kämpfen; Kampf, Streit
file Ordner, Datei
find finden, suchen
fine gut, schön, fein
finish Ende; (be)enden
fire Feuer
firm Firma
first erste/r/s, zuerst
first name Vorname
fly fliegen
follow (be)folgen
following folgende
food Essen, Nahrung
foot Fuß
forever für immer
forget vergessen
form Form, Formular
free kostenlos, frei
freedom Freiheit
French französisch
friend Freund/in
friendly freund(schaft)lich
from von
fruit Obst, Frucht
full voll
fun Spaß
funny komisch, merkwürdig
future Zukunft; (zu)künftig

G
game Spiel
German deutsch
gift Geschenk
girl Mädchen
girlfriend Freundin
give geben
glass Glas
go gehen, fahren
go away weggehen
go to work arbeiten gehen
good gut
grade Note
granddad Großvater
grandma Großmutter
great groß(artig), toll
green grün
grey grau
group Gruppe
guess Annahme; raten, schätzen
guitar Gitarre

H
hair Haar(e)
half Hälfte; halb
ham Schinken
hand Hand
happiness Glück
happy glücklich, froh, zufrieden
hard schwer, hart
hate hassen, nicht mögen
have to do etwas tun müssen
head Kopf
hear hören
help Hilfe; helfen
here hier
hero Held
high hoch, groß; äußerst
holiday Ferien, Urlaub
home Zuhause, Heim; nach Hause
homework Hausaufgaben
hope hoffen; Hoffnung
hospital Krankenhaus
hot heiß, warm
hour Stunde
house Haus
how wie
huge riesig
hungry hungrig
husband (Ehe-)Mann

I
idea Idee, Gedanke
ill krank
important wichtig
include enthalten, umfassen
including einschließlich
indoors innen
information Auskunft, Information(en)
inside innerhalb, drinnen

interview Interview, Vorstellungsgespräch; interviewen
into in ... hinein
invite einladen
Irish irisch
Italian italienisch

J
job Arbeit, Stelle
joke Witz
just einfach, nur, genau

K
key Schlüssel, Taste
kiss küssen; Kuss
kitchen Küche
know kennen, wissen

L
language Sprache
large groß, umfangreich
last letzte/r/s, zuletzt
late spät
latest neueste
laugh lachen
leader Leiter/in, Anführer
learn lernen, erfahren
least wenigstens
leave (ver)lassen
left linke/r/s, links; übrig
lesson Lektion, Unterrichtsstunde
letter Brief, Buchstabe
life Leben
lift Fahrstuhl, Aufzug
like (ähnlich) wie; mögen, gern tun
line Leitung
lipstick Lippenstift
list Liste; auflisten, notieren
listen zuhören
little klein, wenig
live wohnen, leben
long lang
longer länger
look Blick; (aus)sehen, blicken
lost verloren
loud laut
love Liebe; lieben, sehr gern mögen
lovely schön, hübsch, reizend
low niedrig
luck Glück

lucky glücklich
lunchtime Mittagspause

M
machine Maschine
mad verrückt, toll
magazine Zeitschrift
main reason Hauptgrund
make machen
male männlich
man Mann, Mensch
mark markieren
market Markt
maybe vielleicht
meal Essen, Mahlzeit
meat Fleisch
meet (zusammen)treffen, begegnen
message Mitteilung, Nachricht
metre Meter
milk Milch
miss verpassen, vermissen
month Monat
more mehr
morning Morgen
most meist
motorbike Motorrad
mountain bike Mountainbike
move (sich) bewegen, umziehen
much viel
mushroom Pilz

N
nationality Staatsangehörigkeit
necessary nötig
need Bedarf; brauchen, benötigen
nervous nervös
nice(ly) schön, nett
night Nacht
nightlife Nachtleben
nobody niemand
noise Geräusch, Lärm
noisy laut, geräuschvoll
north Nord(en)
northern nördlich
nose Nase
note Notiz; beachten, notieren
nothing nichts
now nun, jetzt
number Nummer, Zahl
nursery nurse Kindergärtnerin

O
of course natürlich, selbstverständlich
office Büro, Amt
old alt
older älter
only nur, einzig
open öffnen, beginnen; offen
opinion Meinung, Einschätzung
order Reihenfolge, Ordnung
other andere/r/s
outdoors draußen
outside außer(halb)
over (vor)über

P
pairwork Partnerarbeit
paper Papier, Zeitung
parents Eltern
part Teil, Rolle
past vorbei, nach; Vergangenheit
pay (be)zahlen
people Personen, Menschen
per day pro Tag
perhaps vielleicht, eventuell
phone Telefon; anrufen
phone call (Telefon-)Anruf
phone number Telefonnummer
piano Klavier
pickle eingelegtes Gemüse
picture Bild
piece Stück
place Stelle, Platz; setzen, stellen
plan Plan; planen
plant Pflanze
play spielen
please bitte
pleased zufrieden
point Punkt; Komma
policeman Polizist
poor arm, schlecht, mangelhaft
portion Portion, Menge, Anteil
postcard Postkarte
practice Übung
prefer vorziehen, bevorzugen
pretty hübsch; ziemlich
prince Prinz
probably wahrscheinlich
problem Problem
program (Computer-)Programm
pub Kneipe, Gaststätte
pull ziehen

pupil Schüler/in
push schieben, drücken
put setzen, stellen, legen

Q
question Frage
quiet still, ruhig
quite ziemlich, ganz

R
rain Regen; regnen
read lesen
real echt, wirklich
reality Realität, Wirklichkit
really wirklich, eigentlich, tatsächlich
recognize erkennen
red rot
relax (sich) erholen
remember sich erinnern, daran denken
rice Reis
rich reich
right rechts, rechte/r/s, **richtig;** Recht
ring Ring; klingeln, anrufen
road (Land-)Straße
role Rollen
room Zimmer, Raum
round Runde; rund

S
sad traurig
sale (Schluss-)Verkauf
salt Salz
same gleiche/r/s, der-, die-, dasselbe
scan (ein)scannen
school Schule
sea See
seat Sitz(platz), Stuhl
second zweite/r/s; Sekunde
secret Geheimnis
secretary Sekretär/in
section Abschnitt
see sehen
seem scheinen
sell (sich) verkaufen
send senden, schicken
serve dienen
set setzen
several etliche, einige, mehrere
shock Schock
shoe Schuh

shop Laden, Geschäft; einkaufen
shopping mall Einkaufsstraße, Kaufhauspassage
short kurz, klein
should solle/n, sollte/n
shout schreien, rufen
show zeigen
showbiz party Party mit Promis aus der Showbranche
sick krank
side Seite
silent still, Stumm
silly dumm, doof, albern, lächerlich
sing singen
singer Sänger/in
sister Schwester
sit sitzen
ski Ski (fahren)
sleep Schlaf; schlafen
slow(ly) langsam
small klein
smile lächeln; Lächeln
snow Schnee; schneien
soft weich
some einige, etwas
someone jemand
something etwas
sometimes manchmal
son Sohn
soon bald
sort Sorte, Art
soup Suppe
south Süden
Spain Spanien
Spanish spanisch
speak sprechen, reden
speaker Redner/in
special besondere
spell buchstabieren, schreiben
start Beginn; anfangen, starten, beginnen
stay Aufenthalt; bleiben
stop Halt; (an) halten, aufhören (mit)
store Laden, Geschäft
story Erzählung, Geschichte
strange fremd, seltsam
street Straße
strong stark, kräftig
student Student/in, Lernende/r
stupid dumm
subject (Schul-)Fach, Thema
sugar Zucker
suggest vorschlagen, andeuten
summer Sommer

sun Sonne
supermarket Supermarkt
sure freilich, sicher(lich)
surname Nach-, Familienname
surprise Überraschung; überraschen
swim schwimmen

T
table Tisch, Tabelle
take nehmen, bringen, dauern
talk Gespräch, Unterhaltung; sprechen, reden
tea Tee
teach unterrichten, lehren
teacher Lehrer/in
teen(age) Teen(age), Jugendliche/r
tell sagen, erzählen
than als
these diese
thing Sache, Ding, Gegenstand
think denken, meinen, finden, glauben
though obwohl, doch
ticket Karte, Fahrschein
time Zeit, Mal
today heute
together zusammen
tomorrow morgen
tonight heute Abend/Nacht
top Spitze, Gipfel
topic Thema
total(ly) völlig, (ins)gesamt
tourism Tourismus
town Stadt
toy Spielzeug
train Zug
trainee Auszubildende/r
training Training, Übung
translate übersetzen, -tragen
transport Transport, Verkehr
travel Reisen; reisen, fahren
tree Baum
true richtig, wahr
truth Wahrheit
try versuchen, probieren
type erfassen, tippen; Art
typical typisch

U
understand verstehen, begreifen
unhappy unglücklich
until bis

use benutzen, verwenden; Verwendung
useful nützlich
usual(ly) normalerweise, gewöhnlich, meistens

V

village Dorf
visit Besuch; besuchen, besichtigen

W

walk Spaziergang; (zu Fuß) gehen
want wollen
wash waschen
watch sehen, beobachten
watch TV fernsehen
water Wasser
way Weg, Methode, Art (und Weise)
weather Wetter
webpage Internetseite
week Woche
weekend Wochenende
west West(en)
what was, welche/r/s
where wo(hin)
will Wille; werde(n), wollen
win gewinnen, siegen
window Fenster
without ohne
woman Frau
wonder sich fragen, wundern
wood Holz, Wald
word Wort
work Arbeit, Werk; funktionieren, arbeiten
worker Arbeiter/in
workout Training
workshop Werkstatt
world Welt
written geschrieben, schriftlich
wrong falsch

Y

year Jahr
yellow gelb
yesterday gestern
young jung

GEOGRAPHICAL WORDS

Africa Afrika
Albania Albanien
Australia Australien
Austria Österreich
Canada Kanada
China China
Èire *(irisch für:)* Irland
Europe Europa
European Union Europäische Union
France Frankreich
Germany Deutschland
Great Britain Großbritannien
Greece Griechenland
Iceland Island
India Indien
Ireland Irland
Italy Italien
Japan Japan
LA (Los Angeles) Los Angeles
Lake Constance Bodensee
Mexico Mexiko
New Zealand Neuseeland
Russia Russland
Scotland Schottland
Singapore Singapur
Spain Spanien
Switzerland *(die)* Schweiz
the Netherlands die Niederlande
United Kingdom (UK) Vereinigtes Königreich
United States (US) Vereinigte Staaten
Washington DC Washington DC

IRREGULAR VERBS

be – was/were – been sein
beat – beat – beaten schlagen, besiegen
become – became – become werden
begin – began – begun anfangen, beginnen
break – broke – broken brechen
build – built – built bauen
burn – burnt/burned – burnt/burned (ver)brennen
buy – bought – bought kaufen
come – came – come kommen
cut – cut – cut schneiden
do – did – done tun, machen
draw – drew – drawn zeichnen
dream – dreamt – dreamt träumen
drink – drank – drunk trinken
drive – drove – driven fahren
eat – ate – eaten essen
fall – fell – fallen fallen
feed – fed – fed füttern, ernähren
feel – felt – felt (sich) fühlen, empfinden
fight – fought – fought kämpfen
find – found – found finden
fit – fit/fitted – fitted passen, sitzen; anbringen
fly – flew – flown fliegen
forget – forgot – forgotten vergessen
get – got – got *(AE gotten)* bekommen
give – gave – given geben
go – went – gone gehen, fahren
grow – grew – grown wachsen
hang – hung – hung hängen
have – had – had haben
hear – heard – heard hören
hide – hid – hidden (sich) verstecken
hit – hit – hit schlagen
hold – held – held halten, festhalten
keep – kept – kept behalten
know – knew – known kennen, wissen
lay – laid – laid legen
lead – led – led führen
learn – learnt/learned – learnt/learned lernen
leave – left – left abfahren, verlassen, weggehen
let – let – let lassen
lie – lay – lain liegen
light – lit – lit anzünden, beleuchten
lose – lost – lost verlieren
make – make – make machen
mean – meant – meant meinen, bedeuten
meet – met – met treffen
offset – offset – offset ausgleichen
pay – paid – paid bezahlen

put – put – put setzen, stellen, legen
quit – quit/quitted – quit/quitted verlassen, aufhören
read – read – read lesen
ride – rode – ridden reiten, fahren
rise – rose – risen (an)steigen
ring – rang – rung läuten, klingeln
run – ran – run laufen, rennen
say – said – said sagen
see – saw – seen sehen
seek – sought – sought suchen
sell – sold – sold verkaufen
send – sent – sent senden, schicken
set – set – set setzen, stellen
shake – shook – shaken schütteln
show – showed – shown zeigen
shrink – shrank – shrunk schrumpfen, verdichten; zurückschrecken
shut – shut – shut schließen
sing – sang – sung singen
sink – sank/sunk – sunk sinken
sit – sat – sat sitzen
sleep – slept – slept schlafen
smell – smelt/smelled – smelt/smelled riechen
speak – spoke – spoken sprechen
spell – spelt/spelled – spelt/spelled buchstabieren
spend – spent – spent ausgeben, verbringen
spin – spun – spun sich drehen, herumwirbeln
stand – stood – stood stehen
steal – stole – stolen stehlen
stride – strode – stridden schreiten
strive – strove/strived – striven/strived streben (nach)
swim – swam – swum schwimmen
take – took – taken nehmen
teach – taught – taught unterrichten, beibringen
tell – told – told sagen, erzählen
think – thought – thought denken
thrive – thrived – thrived florieren
throw – threw – thrown werfen
thrust – thrust – thrust stoßen
understand – understood – understood verstehen
wake – woke/waked – woken/waked aufwachen, wecken
wear – wore – worn tragen
win – won – won gewinnen
withhold – withheld – withheld verweigern, vorenthalten
write – wrote – written schreiben

MONEY QUIZ

Say which statements are true for you.

1. I know exactly how much I should spend each week and I try not to go over that amount.
2. I try to save 10% of my money (pocket money or what I earn) every month.
3. When I get extra money, for example for my birthday, I put it into a savings account.
4. I use vouchers and special offers whenever I can.
5. Almost every time I buy a big item, I check different shops for the best price.
6. I don't eat out more than twice a week.
7. I collect my receipts and check them carefully to see what I've bought.
8. I have given food/money to a needy person in the last two weeks.
9. I have debts which I know I can pay.
10. I have debts which I know I can't pay.

Evaluation

Statements 1–8

If you answered YES to all of these statements, you handle your money very well.

If you answered YES to up to 4 of these statements, you are on the way to handling your money quite well. Share your ideas with other people in the class and listen to their ideas.

If you answered YES to fewer than 3 statements, you should think a bit more about what you do with your money.

Statements 9–10

If you answered YES to statement 9, you may want to re-think the way you handle your money.

If you answered YES to statement 10, think hard about how you handle your money.

USEFUL PHRASES

Wie sagt man's am besten auf Englisch?	How do you say it in English?
Was für eine Arbeit machst du?	What is your job?
Ich arbeite in einem sozialen Assistenzberuf.	I work in health and social care.
Ich bin Sozialassistent/in/ Pflegeassistent/in.	I am a social care assistant / health care assistant.
Ich begleite Menschen in ihrem Alltag.	I look after people in their day-to-day life.
Ich arbeite in / einer Kinderkrippe / in einem Kindergarten / in einem Schulhort.	I work in a crèche / in a nursery / at an after-school club.
Ich kümmere mich um Kinder.	I look after children.
Ich arbeite in einem Altenheim.	I work in a residential home for the elderly.
Ich bin verantwortlich dafür, dass es den Bewohnern gut geht.	I am responsible for the welfare of the residents.
Ich arbeite in einem Wohnheim für Menschen mit Mehrfachbehinderungen.	I work in a residential home for people with complex disabilities / complex special needs.
Ich kümmere mich um Menschen mit Behinderungen.	I look after people with disabilities / special needs.

Achtung! It is important to talk about 'people with disabilities / special needs' and NOT 'disabled people'. The disability does not define the person! Many people are offended by the term 'disabled people'.

Vokabelliste	Vocabulary list
Wie beschreibt man pflegebedürftige Menschen?	How do we talk about people who need health and social care services?
Frau mit eingeschränkter Mobilität/ Beweglichkeit	a woman with limited mobility
bettlägeriger Mensch	a person who is confined to bed
gehbehinderter Mann	a man who has walking problems

taub	deaf
gehörlos	deaf-mute
blind	blind
stumm	mute
hörbeeinträchtigter Mensch	a person with impaired hearing
sehbeeinträchtigter Mensch	a person with impaired vision
sprachbeeinträchtigter Mensch	a person with impaired speech
demenzkranker Mensch	a person who suffers from dementia
Kind mit Lernschwierigkeiten	a child with learning difficulties
Mensch mit einer Behinderung	a person with a disability
Mensch mit besonderen Bedürfnissen	a person with special needs

Aktivitäten	**Activities**
Kindern Geschichten vorlesen	to read stories to children
Kindern Lieder vorsingen	to sing songs to children
mit Kindern Spiele spielen	to play games with children
mit Kindern Spaziergänge machen	to go for a walk with children
ältere Menschen bei der Körperpflege unterstützen	to help elderly people to wash and dress
älteren Menschen bei Bewegungsübungen helfen	to help elderly people to do physical exercises
Menschen mit besonderen Bedürfnissen das Essen anreichen	to help people with special needs to eat
mit älteren Menschen basteln	to do arts and crafts with elderly people
mit älteren Menschen Tagesausflüge machen	to go on day trips with elderly people
kochen/einkaufen	to do the cooking / to do the shopping
Wäsche waschen	to do the washing / the laundry
Mahlzeiten vorbereiten	to prepare meals

Baustein Soziales Bildquellenverzeichnis

RF-Fotos:
Alamy: S. 35/1/ImageSourcePink/IS605, S. 36/3/ImageSourceBlack/IS588, S. 44/ImageSourceBlack/IS-200512, S. 46/2/picturesbyrob/tf3, S. 53/1/ImageSourceBlack/IS647, S. 66/2, S. 66/1

J. Frey: S. 68/1, S. 73/1, S. 73/2;

Scott Louden Photography: S. 68/6

Istockphoto: S. 5/4, S. 41/2, S. 41/3

Shutterstock: S. 5/5, S. 10, S. 20/1, S. 23/2, S. 24, S. 29/2, S. 29/3, S. 36/4, S. 36/5, S. 40/1 Shutterstock.com/sanneberg, S. 40/2, S. 46/1, S. 50/2, S. 51, S. 52/1, S. 52/2, S. 53/2, S. 53/5 Shutterstock.com/annscreations, S. 53/6 Shutterstock.com/FamVeld, S 66/3, S. 68/2, S. 68/5, S. 78/1, S. 78/2;

RM-Fotos:
Alamy: S. 22/C. Wilton, S. 23/1/A. Holt, S. 29/1/D. Green, S. 29/4/D. Hancock, S. 35/2/J. Powell, S. 36/1, S. 36/2/D. Grossman, S. 40/3/Horizon, S. 41/D. MacDonald, S. 45/3/J. Wiedel, S. 50/1/dalekhelen, S. 53/3/P. Doyle, S. 53/4/J. Wiedel

Cinetext: S. 20/3/Allstar;

Fotofinder: S. 5/1/Keystone/Houzzer; S. 5/2/hasskarl.de/D. Hasskarl; S. 5/3/Lichtblick/G. Frebel; S. 5/6/Joker/R. Gerard; S. 12/FotexMedien/Susa; S. 32/F1 Online/ableimages; S. 45/1/A1PIX/EMA; S. 45/2/Fotoarchiv; S. 45/4/P. Hympendahl; S. 60/1/Caro/Teschner, S. 60/2/Caro/Trappe; S. 68/3/Allesalltag; S. 68/4/Allesalltag,

Picture Alliance: S. 20/2/W. Langenstrassen, S. 40/epd, S. 56/Osports